Also by Ben Tanzer

Orphans
Lost in Space
The New York Stories
SEX AND DEATH

BE COOL

a memoir (sort of)

by

BEN TANZER

DOCK STREET PRESS

SEATTLE

www.dockstreetpress.com

Cover photo by Jacob S. Knabb.

Dock Street Press and colophon are registered
trademarks of Dock Street Press

ISBN:978-0-9910657-8-3

Printed in the U.S.A.

For Jim Carroll, Adam "MCA" Yauch,
Ned Vizzini and Joey Ramone.

CONTENTS

The 1980's

The 1990's

2000 –PRESENT

BE COOL

PREFACE

It's certainly possible that I'm writing you today because I was so greatly moved by the outcome of Obergefell v. Hodges.

Not that I ever vowed not to marry until everyone had the right to do so, which at best, may make me look like a fair-weather groom to be, and at worst like I am merely looking to ride the wave of gay marriage euphoria so as to satisfy my need to fit in and be cool.

Which is something you should know about me before we go any further: while I have been prescient regarding any number of social trends—baggy jeans, superhero fanboy love, Moscow Mules and vintage T-shirts advertising obscure restaurants, coffee shops and pool halls, to name just a few—I am also more than willing to follow trends as well—the Lumbersexual lifestyle for example— and if you could learn to embrace it going into this that would rock.

You also need to know, that I am happily married, and in a heterosexual manner at that, i.e., my wife is female, and she is lovely, and to be clear, this isn't about her, it's about me.

On a scale ranging from man buns to baggy jeans my love for her falls squarely in the middle of the continuum—slightly higher on the days she brings home little chocolate donuts—and the only reason she doesn't represent the far end of the scale herself is that I have loved baggy jeans longer than I have loved her and loyalty is very important to me.

But again, this is not about her, it's about me, and my hope is that she will be able to live with us on the compound regardless.

Did I mention the compound?

Sorry, I'm getting ahead of myself.

I do that too sometimes.

The compound doesn't actually exist beyond my imagination at this time, but I visualize us living in a small enclave of low-slung stucco bungalows or ranch style homes—I'm super flexible on the bungalow versus ranch style front—which have back decks steps from the beach.

How do you feel about the beach by the way?

Do you know what that is? If you don't, it's a land mass generally comprised of sand, salt air, ocean and waves.

The part regarding the ocean is especially important to me, and I say this because my Chicago brothers and sisters—who I love dearly, though not as much as baggy jeans mind you—will insist that I live near the beach now, which technically I do, but it's the beach on Lake Michigan and you see where this is going right?

I hope so, because if this whole marriage thing is going to work, I will expect that you're just going to know what I mean about something whether I say it or not, because if it's obvious to me, it will be obvious to you too.

Anyway, before we get into me and you, or more accurately my expectations of you, and your expectations of me, and our future marriage, all of that, let's finish our discussion about the compound and where it might be located.

Florida could certainly work. Miami is fine, as is Key West. It's just that it's Florida, right? Still, I'm not dismissing the whole state out of hand. A marriage can't work if that's how one deals with conflict.

In fact, please know that I'm not reflexively dogmatic about most things.

That's just not my jam.

I'm pretty laidback really.

Which I suppose isn't exactly true.

I am quite dogmatic about some things, or at least I am quite opposed on a visceral level to some things, for example, anything, or anyone, that oppresses someone's voice or rights, which I suppose is one reason the right to gay marriage has always spoken to me.

As my father used to say, doesn't everyone have the right to suffer equally?

Speaking of my father, you would have liked him, everyone did. He was funny and different. Not that liking him is a deal breaker, and he passed away anyway, which haunts the hell out of me, but actually leaves you with all kinds of leeway on that front no matter what your feeling is about liking him.

My mother is another story though. Liking her is a deal breaker. But I know that you know that already, because that's our thing, right, we know each other.

So anyway, I'll want my mom to live with us on the compound as well, which could be in Florida, though Cape Cod could be fine. I spent a lot of summers there when I was a kid and I always loved it, especially Provincetown, and especially at night – the crowds, the noise, the joy, the constant sense that a party was happening, all of it.

That said, I don't think I really want to do winters any more.

Is that okay?

I guess I've just noticed during the last couple of winters, that I'm happier when the gray skies pass, and the sun starts poking its way through the clouds and into the windows of our apartment. I never thought that the weather had any effect on my mood, but something changed, or maybe I was just always wrong about who I am, or unwilling to accept it, and now I can own up to that, the being wrong, which is healthy, right?

Also though, and let me be transparent for a moment, because that's important in marriage too, right, being transparent, even when what you expose is a little ugly?

Not that this is ugly per se, but even as I am talking about Florida or Cape Cod, and wanting to be flexible, transparent, and all of that, I really do picture the compound being located somewhere in Southern California, though where exactly, I'm definitely flexible about that.

I guess the more I'm writing, the more I'm realizing now how much I loved it out there when I was a kid, because that's another place I spent summers when I got older, Los Angeles in particular, and it has a lot of meaning to me, who I was, what I became, and didn't.

I had my first crush in Los Angeles and my first recorded erection, well, recorded by me anyway. It's not in the official history books for Los Angeles, erections or anything like that.

I did not have my first kiss there, however, and we should note that too, because I probably could have, and may very well of fumbled that, and I'm telling you this, because I want to be vulnerable where and when I can—you're just getting to know me—and being vulnerable in a marriage is important too.

I saw *E. T.*, *Blade Runner* and *Stripes* for the first time in Los Angeles.

I also saw *The Decline of Western Civilization* there, which I kind of hated then, and which you can fault me for today, but that's okay, it's you and me now, and some things are not going to sit well with you.

My wife for example hates *Star Wars*.

Star Wars.

I know, it's crazy, but we've worked through it, because one poor or confused choice does not make for the whole person.

I know you get that though, and I love that about you. But enough about *Star Wars* and my lovely, albeit confused, wife, we're all about Los Angeles here, and so we can't forget Santa Monica Pier or Venice Beach, in all of its dirty, freaker awesomeness.

I guess when I look back, I really felt alive there and I always have since.

Not that I don't feel alive, or lucky, here, now. I have love and work and words, but even as good as I have it, I can see doing the second half of my life differently, and when I think about how all of that might look, one of my models is the artist Raymond Pettibon.

Do you know him?

And I don't want to say that you should know him. I hate it when people say that to me, and that's no way for things to start between us, me saying something to you that I would hate hearing myself.

Still, what you should know is that he's this wonderful artist from Hermosa beach, who came of age in the Los Angeles punk scene of the 1970's and 80's—which yes, I once kind of hated, we've established that—and made zines and art and who lives near the beach in the house he grew-up in, and I don't know if he has a wife or kids, though if I can be frank for a moment, with the economy as it is, my kids may need to live with us on the compound as well, which I hope is okay with you, because there're lovely too, mostly.

But the point is, Raymond Pettibon lives near the beach, and makes art in the morning before moving on to other things in the afternoon, and he's living this creative, punk, Southern Californian beach life that is so not the life I've been living with my 9-5 job, my stress about health insurance and 401(k)s, and what he has, is what I want going forward—more art, more beach, more punk and less worry about structure and everything being taken care of.

All of which may be me projecting what I want onto his life, which may not even truly be his life. And yes, I do project, a lot, but why can't I get-up in the morning, run, write, take care of business—phone calls, meetings, emails, whatever—go surfing, eat tacos, and then who knows what—yoga, more work, movies, drinks—and please note that I do plan to start drinking more often—afternoon drinking I'm thinking—though always in moderation of course.

Anyway, I really think I want to live that life, and I also think you could be there for that.

This does remind me though that there are things about me you should know.

For example, I run, I have to.

I am enthralled with the not just the story of Icarus, but the very idea of Icarus as a thing that explains things, my things anyway.

I love tacos and donuts, and there are lots of good donut and taco joints in Los Angeles, not that I'm pushing that location.

Really.

I also really want to learn how to surf, that's a long-term plan or goal, and it may just be a fantasy, but that can change, right?

And of course at this point, I'm sure it's clear to you that so much of this is about change and transformation and somehow making all of that happen.

You may also be wondering, however, why I need to re-marry to do any of this, and why I want a husband, and while I suppose I really don't, all I can say, is that the heterosexual thing has been great, I'm pretty good at it, and it has certainly worked for me, but I've also been working off of that model for all of these years, and so much in the same way that I've been working off of the 9-5 work model, but want to drop it, I'm also willing to try something new on the orientation front for the next half of my life.

My thinking here, is that my current orientation has worked fine, but why limit myself to what I know, and where I feel safe, because who knows what I may learn or what's possible?

Haven't I done enough of that already?

I should probably take a minute here to sell me some more, or at least make sure you get to know me better, because you may not want to marry me merely because I have some amorphous plan to construct a life that fits my needs and includes art, surfing, tacos and drinking, low-slung stucco bungalows or ranch houses in Southern California, possibly Los Angeles, maybe Hermosa Beach, as well as my wife, mother and children.

So, I will begin by saying that I love hard and I give good hug and I believe that these are real selling points.

I'm also a good listener, something that I get from my mother, and that my wife will certainly attest to.

Did I mention that you will like them?

Good.

Because I really do give good listen, gladly, and intensely, but I'm not weird about it. Not that being heard feels totally normal either, most people don't have people who are willing to listen to them and from that perspective it will seem weird to you at first.

You'll adjust though, promise.

I like to do the laundry. I've always done it for myself, and those around me, so that's covered.

Dishes are also cool with me, vacuuming too.

You should know upfront though, that I may not notice that the house needs to be vacuumed, or that the bathroom needs to be cleaned.

I'm not always good at that, the noticing part.

If someone points it out though, I'm on it, ninja-style.

I'm not terribly inclined to cook either, but I do well in the area of breakfast.

I'm happy to stay home or go out and I can get along with anybody you want to go out with. I will figure out what they like to talk about and I will be happy to talk about that.

I do have compulsions, however, and this may not bother you, but you should still know about them.

So, while I like to do the laundry, I also need it to be folded and neat when it's done and then you can't mess with the piles before they're properly put away, that drives me a little crazy.

I check the locks a couple of time before I go to sleep

and the alarm clock as well, I can never quite settle down without doing so.

I will try to fix things for you when you are sad or frustrated, and I've only learned recently that people don't always want their shit fixed for them, but I'm getting better at that.

I'm missing some finger tips, one really, and some padding in another, and I don't think anyone ever notices this, but you should know.

I was assaulted once in New York City, and I think the trauma of that has mostly passed, but there are times, when people seem especially aggressive or the shadows get weird, that my heart starts racing and I wonder if I'm going to need to fight, and then I think I kind of want to fight, and then I settle down. It mostly happens in my head, and you may not pick up on it at all, but again, you should know what you're getting into.

Also, I binge watch television, though everyone does now, and I binge read, always have; and I still binge drink at times, which I'm not super proud of. I'm a pleasant drunk, I think, but unless I focus on having just two drinks, which I'm pretty good at doing these days, two can still quickly become ten or more. It's infrequent and probably will have no negative effect on you, but again you should know all of this.

Transparency, yo.

And I have to run.

I know that I mentioned that already, but let that wash over you anyway, because it's not about exercise, and that's important for you to know, now, upfront.

It's a need, a corrective, a way of life.

I think about it all of the time, just as I think about writing, when and how will I do it, and if I can do both first thing in the morning, all the better, for all of us, because it calms the constant need I have to figure out when I will do so next and what it will look like.

All of which is to say, that the Los Angeles model as I currently visualize it will alleviate some of the craziness around all of this, but you still have to take it all in and decide it's for you.

Again, my wife and my mom will be joining us on the compound, and maybe my kids.

There will be surfing, and tacos, running, Icarus, and sand, punk music and art.

But there will also be love, lots of it, and joy, and I honestly think it will all be a lot of fun.

So, please take a moment to think about all of this. It's a big step, but if you're ready, I can be too.

Cool?

Cool,

Ben Tanzer
Chicago, 2016

THE 1980's

WHEN I WAS TWELVE

When I was twelve I was endlessly running around. I ran down Moore Avenue until the sidewalk ends to get to the school bus in the morning and then all during lunch on the soccer field across from school—through the dirt and the dust as we chased one another around, swearing, tackling the slowest amongst us, and trying to escape the older kids who hunted us down in packs and then punched our arms until they were numb.

When lunch was done I ran down the hall to class, gliding across the flecked floors, the murky fluorescent lighting swamp-like and hazy.

I ran from Spanish class, where I recited my lessons, no hint of an accent; to gym, where I dutifully meandered up and down the basketball court attempting lay-ups I could not hit.

I would eventually find myself in math class and staring at the clock, which moved so very slow—so much slower than I did certainly.

The clock hung above a sign that read *Time will pass, will you?*

I might have stopped to contemplate the implications of that question, but the bell would ring before I could and I was off again, tearing down the hall and out the door, the end of the school day finally upon me.

I moved quickly from school to bus to home and out again, stopping only long enough to change into shorts and a T-shirt, my brow already damp, the hair wet behind my ears.

Then I was gone, and on the run again, my canvas Nikes slapping the pavement as I ran to track practice.

I began by heading down the driveway that took so long to clear with our rusty shovels when it snowed, looking briefly both ways before cruising across the street and curling around the left side of the Stanley's house.

I flew past the tree they would later cut down for their new driveway, barreling through their backyard and towards the hill behind their back porch, where I would pause, hold my breath, and recite a short prayer before plunging through the tree branches, covering my eyes, sliding on the rocks and dirt and roots, my fingertips brushing the path, then bounding across the patio of the house behind theirs, dodging the mysterious wire that ran along the garage—I was sure that if I caught my hand on it and it came loose, the house would blow-up and it would all be my fault.

Having dodged the wire, I was free to explode onto their driveway and across Overbrook Drive where I would start to madly pump my arms as I hit the dip in the next backyard before jumping over their hedges.

I couldn't fall there, no time for that. I would lift my feet above the branches even as I slammed into their lawn still at full speed—palms flat and horizontal to the ground for balance—already crossing Aldrich, no longer looking for traffic, and heading towards the Johnson's house.

As I went past the Johnson's kitchen I would wave to Mrs. Johnson before twisting around their garage and leaping into oblivion through the narrow opening in the bushes behind their house.

I would land breathlessly moments later in Joe Leonard's backyard, a move that sometimes caused my knees to buckle, but never slowed me down, not even when the lawn was wet and I sank with each step into the mossy grass, the mud spraying the back of my shirt as I powered towards the Leonard's front yard.

I had no time to think about mud though as I continued past the Leonard's and onto Kendall, turning hard to the right, my arms and legs a blur.

I was flying now, the backyard of Jennifer Jones' house already a memory—she of the ten brothers and sisters, so many really they could not be told apart—though that is also where I would someday kiss Terry Mann at midnight on her birthday, a moment so very electric and filled with so much teen longing, it would linger for time immemorial.

And then just prior to the downhill stretch on Kendall, there was this moment, just a moment mind you, where the world seemed to disappear as I crested that last piece of flat road before reaching Brookfield Road.

I would slow here, bracing for the sudden appearance of the world's end—thoughts of Icarus entering my head—but the world didn't end, and there was Brookfield, where I would make an abrupt left, nearly tipping over from the force of the turn.

I was out of breath now, so very tired.

My lungs were heaving.

My legs were heavy.

The soles of my feet were burning.

I wore no socks when I ran like this and I could feel the skin on the bottom of my feet grinding against the insoles of my sneakers with each bump, rock and stumble.

And then I was on Brookfield.

It was at this point that I could see the track for the first time and now my arms were really pumping as I leaned into the wind and whipped by the crossing guard my younger brother Adam always fought with—the one without the nose, who wore a windbreaker no matter what time of year it was and always left candy on the mailbox for us, BB Bats and Laffy Taffy, Kit Kats and Bazooka gum, the comic strip and fortune awaiting those who were patient enough to slow down and open the wrapper with care.

That was not me though.

No patience here.

No slowing down.

I was already across Vestal Avenue at this point and heading down the driveway leading to my old elementary school—the one rumored to sink an inch per year because they built it on a swamp—now veering past the playground where we used to throw snowballs at passing cars before racing down the hill on our sleds and hiding behind the slide shaped like a rocket ship—and then moving past the school itself—and the little league field—and hanging yet another left as I drove towards the field in the middle of the track—where everyone was gathering for practice—the place where I learned to ride a bike, my dad holding me steady as I rolled across the grass, all intensity and fear, seeking some semblance of balance and self-preservation.

And once there, I stretched, kind of, but only briefly, because soon I was on the track itself for our warm-up run and I was moving again, always moving, joining the masses, and lazily jogging around the track, weaving from lane to lane.

We jabbered away, checking-out the girls, especially

Ali Burnett, who I loved, and who ran all straight-backed and lovely, like a dancer, her long brown hair braided and pulled into a ponytail.

The ponytail bounced on her back with each stride, catching the late day sun with every undulation, and mesmerizing to the adolescent eye.

The track was a sacred place, a safe place, a second home, and now that I was on it, I could finally slow down a little, catch my breath and slough off the day's events.

The real world—school, parents, the endless effort to be cool—may have constantly encroached on me everywhere else, but not there, not on the track.

There I was a god, untouchable and all-powerful.

And for that I was, and am, thankful.

THERE WILL BE BLOOD

It is 1980, I am twelve years old and there is so much blood.

Not mine, but my younger brother Adam's, who is lying on the floor at my feet, crumpled and stunned, and cradling his head in his little hands.

It's New Year's Eve, we are in Provincetown at a hotel and our parents have gone out to dinner.

The room is typical of those many of us stayed in during that era—Bob Ross look-a-like paintings of the sea shore; rough, Brillo-aspiring blankets; brown, faux wood paneling; a television with ten somewhat fuzzy channels, three of which are the hotel's own; and a rug that is moist to the touch, but not so much as to leave your socks wet.

Our mom and dad told us not to jump from bed to bed while they were out, much less fight in mid-air between the beds.

But it's all we've been doing all trip, and if there has been the sense that a crash was inevitable, it has somehow been avoided until now.

Now being the operative word, because we may have been told not to jump, but it was too tempting, and too beautiful, and Adam has just fallen short.

Like Icarus, he was aloft, only to have his wings melt, leaving·him hurtling towards the sea, ever spiraling, the ocean spray hitting him in the face as he descended for all eternity.

Then nothing, except for silence and blood, and shock, both his and mine.

I know I have to do something. I could call the front desk. Or Nappy's, the restaurant my parents are at, maybe the police, a hospital.

But none of these things seem like the correct choice. What does seem like the right choice is to go get my parents, on my own, and on foot.

Though not just by foot, I will run to them.

I tell Adam to sit tight and that I will be right back with our mother and father.

He doesn't respond.

I lace up my running shoes and head out into the night.

———

The air is salty, crisp and inky dark.

This isn't the summer Provincetown where the night is filled with packs of boys dressed in leather who follow Adam and I as we go to meet our parents after wandering the streets; where music plays everywhere, pulsating and full of kinetic energy; where every other storefront is a souvenir or T-shirt shop selling cans of Cape Cod air, and Spiritus Pizza, the Penny Patch, and the Army-Navy store, filled with its ancient scuba gear, are always jammed with tourists; where rainbow flags flutter from every building; and there is life, so much life, and so much joy with every stop.

This is winter, and even on New Year's Eve, the people on the streets are few, except for the drunken guy who yells, "Happy New Year's" at me as he and another guy stumble by, and I think, "Happy New Year's for who man, because it's not happy for me and my brother?"

And what must Adam be thinking at this point, laying on the floor of our room, alone, scared, and far from home, as he wonders whether keeping his hands clasped tightly around his head will keep his brains from spilling out onto the rug as he awaits my return?

Not that I'm really thinking about any of that.

Because while I am worried about Adam, what I'm truly thinking about is me, and how I'm saving the day, and that

11

feeling of triumph is what drives me towards Nappy's.

Well that, and the certainty that I will be recognized for my actions.

You see, I'm also thinking about the magazine *Boy's Life*.

Do you remember *Boy's Life*?

It was, and is, *the* scout magazine, not that I was a scout.

I thought about it, the scout thing, but it didn't stick. I didn't care about knots, camping trips, Jamborees, or fat dads with red necks and too tight polo shirts tucked into their polyester, pseudo-polyester football coach shorts.

What did I care about?

What I cared about were books and running, and girls, and that was pretty much it, except that I also cared about being noticed, and being cool, and finding a way to be heroic and larger than life was a clearly a means for getting there.

Which brings us back to *Boy's Life*, a magazine, which despite its religious leanings, something I happily overlooked, spoke to me as much *Dynamite*, *Teen Beat*, and *Sport* did.

Exactly why its voice beckoned was not entirely clear to me then, but now I know it was the picture of normalcy it projected, and what qualified as mainstream and domestic. I didn't have that. I had parents who loved me and showed-up at every game, took us on trips and made sure we had dinner together every Friday night.

But they also went to protests, ate meals at the empty Middle-Eastern restaurant, and generally acted way too ethnic for my upstate town. What they didn't do was watch sports, or drink, or hang out at the Jewish Community Center, much less the Country Club. My dad was an artist and he rode his bike everywhere and my mom was therapist and worked late. None of which actually embarrassed me. Even at an early age I knew they were cool, but I still wanted nothing to do with it, them, or whatever we were. Mostly, I didn't want to be weird. I wanted to be normal, even if I don't remember thinking that in any conscious way.

And *Boy's Life* portrayed a picture of what a kind of normal looked like, or could look like, boys going to scout meetings and talking about Jesus, and everybody looking happy as they were doing so. Which is also not to say I wasn't happy, I don't remember that anyway, it's just that I wanted to be part of a community like the one portrayed in *Boy's Life*.

I just didn't want the *Scout* part getting in the way.

I also knew, however, even if it wasn't totally conscious, that I wanted to be more than all of that too. I wanted to be among the normals, wherever they were, but I also wanted to be recognized as still being something special among them.

Hence my particular fascination with "A True Story of Scouts in Action," an illustrated feature in *Boy's Life* which highlighted great feats of heroism by kids just like me, though not like me exactly, but my age certainly.

The episode that still lingers with me was titled "Fall From a 40-foot Cliff."

It portrays the story of a scout who saves a friend, who, well, you will see this coming, has fallen from a 40-foot cliff.

The colors are terribly vibrant, the friend is falling in his bright red sweater, hands aloft, and the hero is wearing a blue jean jacket, his scout neckerchief loosely tied around his neck.

The hero calms his friend, stops the bleeding, and splints his leg with branches, a belt, and that amazing scout neckerchief.

Why couldn't I be that kid?

I could, except for the fact that apparently I could not. For, isn't it true that I hadn't stopped to calm my brother before I left to get my parents?

It was.

And wasn't it also true that I had not bothered to try and stop the bleeding?

That is true as well, though in my defense, I was not a

scout and did not have a neckerchief at my disposal.

But I did stop to splint Adam's head at least, right?

I don't even know if that's possible, but no, not remotely.

However, despite all of that, did I think about the heroic boy highlighted in "Fall From a 40-Foot Cliff," as I ran, and also kind of think that could be me?

I did, all the way to Nappy's.

Did I also think about how they would illustrate my feature—a larger-than-life image of me in full stride, brow furrowed, splashed across the page, the smell of salt so distinct it would distract the reader from the abject selfishness otherwise running roughshod throughout the piece?

I did that as well.

But were my parents at the restaurant when I got there?

They were not, not at all.

For several summers during my teen years I mowed lawns, picked weeds, cut brush, hated myself for not knowing a better way to earn money, and managed the endless tedium and self-hatred by picturing myself being interviewed on *Late Night with David Letterman*.

What I was being interviewed about was beyond me then, and remains so now. At some point it may have involved the vague idea of writing, something that didn't seem any less improbable to me than getting on the show itself.

It was all fantasy, though it was also a need, and what I know, is that Dave and I laughed and laughed as our brilliance was wordlessly splashed across the screen for the whole world to see and consume.

I was having a moment, and it was spectacular, and while said moment was based on no discernible action I was aware of, I had seized it, just as I once believed I had all those years before when I went out into the night to save Adam.

Which for the record, was in fact an actual action, albeit, a largely misguided one.

When I got back to the hotel, my parents were already there, and Adam was being attended to by paramedics who then took him to a local hospital where they could stitch-up his head.

It turns out that someone had heard him moaning on the floor of our room and called the front desk. They had in turn called for an ambulance, and then located my parents after Adam told them where they were.

No one asked me why I made the decision to leave Adam and run off into the night. He was safe, and apparently that was all that mattered.

I never apologized to him for that—my bout of hubris, and my trip to the sun—but I hope I've made it up to him.

I also never made it into *Boy's Life*, and now that Letterman has retired, my appearance on his show is unlikely to happen either.

I could tell you how none of that is important to me anymore. That getting through every day, working 9-5 so that we can pay our mortgage, getting my children to school on time, and trying to be a good husband, father, son, and brother is enough for me.

That truth be told, I am finally normal, just as I wanted to be, and it rocks, because with all of this going on, who cares about being special anyway?

But I would be lying to you.

I still want to be special. I still crave the sun. And even more than that, part of me still craves someone knowing that I got there, or tried at least.

Am I embarrassed about this?

I am.

But does that need still lead me to make rash decisions that put others at danger?

It does not.

My hubris is now moderated by a sense of responsibility, my wings and wax have been set aside in place of a pen and laptop, and this I truly do consider a kind of victory, even if the need for more still lingers just beyond my reach, and I remain painfully aware that such actions will likely never garner me an illustrated column in *Boy's Life*, much less anywhere else.

THE BIG ONE

I t's not clear that it was a crush, not by any standard
definition I was accustomed to at that time anyway:
See person I'm attracted to.

Find them funny or mysterious, both maybe.

Try to figure out ways to be near them.

Soak-up their energy, and possibly consume them, if
not physically, than metaphysically.

The feeling will be unrequited of course, at least initially. That's certainly my experience.

The feeling will also be followed by a crippling desire that dogs me throughout the day, leaving me restless
at night, and unable to sleep, with little likelihood of that
changing.

So maybe I am incorrect, maybe it was very much
like the crushes I was accustomed to. Maybe what was

different is that this crush was not only unattainable, but male. Though not unattainable because said crush was male, though that was different than my standard crush, but because said crush was Parker Stevenson, and how was that going to work?

It wasn't, I got that, and even then, it wasn't quite sexual anyway, I don't think. It's what he was, and what he represented, a celebrity who seemed like someone I could touch.

Interesting phrasing I suppose.

But Parker Stevenson seemed real, and that's what's important here.

It's important in the same way that the poster of Farah Fawcett which hung on my bedroom wall during those years is important.

You may recall that poster if you spent any time in a 'tween boy's room circa 1980.

Her hair is spectacular, wave after wave of blonde tendrils aloft and crashing across your brain.

Her smile is otherworldly, and unreal, *Blade Runner* unreal, it is like nothing you've ever quite seen before, and you aren't sure you are actually seeing it now.

And then there is the arch of her back and the red bathing suit, anyway enough said.

She too was a crush, but Farah as a crush was more about fantasy, and nothing against Farah, it's just that she was an illusion, untouchable, and possibly a figment of our collective imagination anyway.

And she still might be.

But Parker Stevenson wasn't that, nor was he Shaun Cassidy, with his blonde, pin-up, good looks; pseudo pop-singing prowess; famous half-brother; and general aura of Hollywood royalty.

Of course even then it wasn't just Parker Stevenson's realness and approachability; his good, but not great looks; the welcoming smile, and the pragmatic style he brought to his groundbreaking role as Frank Hardy, one-half of the Hardy Boys, the other half being the aforementioned Shaun Cassidy, the YA lit detective brothers who were prone to referring to mistakes as "boners."

I know, I know, that's base of me to even make that reference, and yet, back then the word boner made me snicker.

Okay, maybe it still does.

And yet, it was even more than all of that.

The world itself was so much smaller then, and this wasn't merely because we had no internet access, or because most of us never flew anywhere, it was because while our access to the larger world was largely driven by television, there were only like three channels to choose from, and so if you liked something, you found yourself really liking it.

It's kind of like having an office crush. Your co-workers comprise a really small sample of the actual opportunities available to you outside of your office, but with the choices so limited, that which you have access to, seems much better than it actually is.

Which is not to bag on *SWAT*, *Charlie's Angels*, *Dallas* or *Fantasy Island*, or any of my co-workers, but again, this is about the real, and compared to the *Hardy Boys* these shows were all cartoons, funny and worthy of our obsessions, but certainly not relatable in any real world way.

Further, and certainly just as important, Parker Stevenson had a column in *Tiger Beat*. You remember *Tiger Beat* don't you? It was the source of all things teen celebrity worship and filled with an ephemera that bordered on gossip and rumor, but never quite crossed-over to outright lies or scandal.

Well, not unless you consider Kristy McNichol and Tatum O'Neal fighting over the affections of Matt Dillon on the set of *Little Darlings* scandalous?

Which you might, which I get, because I am you, and you may just be me, which I suppose I am sorry to hear, sorry for you anyway.

The "me" I am referring to by the way, is the "me" who bee-lined for the magazine rack in the GIANT supermarket on Pennsylvania Avenue near my house growing-up.

And what did Pennsylvania Avenue look like in the late 1970's and early 1980's?

Much like it does now I suppose. There was the GIANT and a series of small houses and apartment buildings, with their peeling paint, sagging front porches; families, young couples, and students; the endless trees towering above them, their branches climbing into the always gray skies; all of which poured onto Vestal Avenue, Pudgie's Pizza, the gas station, the AM/PM, and ultimately the closed bridge which brought you to the Broome County Arena and downtown Binghamton, such as it was.

The magazines themselves were by the bread rack, which abutted the walled-in space where GIANT casually tossed its extra cardboard boxes. An act that led to the formation of a teetering mountain of boxes that was always threatening to topple Jenga-style on to some unsuspecting shopper below, yet never quite did.

It was there, in the shadows of the box mountain, that you could find everything from *Mad* and *Cracked* to *National Enquirer*, TIME, *Newsweek*, and *People*, *Sports Illustrated*, and because this was upstate New York, *Guns & Ammo* and *Soldier of Fortune*.

It was also where you could find me, sweaty and furtive as I read *Tiger Beat*, absorbing its glossy photos, the pages sticky to the touch, the smell of ink heady, and slightly haze-inducing—the experience more akin to sniffing low-grade paint fumes than the high that comes with reading great literature—and consuming *Tiger Beat*'s endless advice columns, including one by none other than the casually sweater-vested Parker Stevenson in all of his grinning glory.

As crushes tend to do, Parker Stevenson had come to represent a way out to me, and while I had no particular feeling at the time about the need to escape Binghamton, I had very particular feelings about remaining obscure, unknown and unwatchable.

Through Parker Stevenson I saw the key to becoming a performer, and while performing per se held no special appeal to me, it did represent a vehicle, a way to becoming whatever he was, someone that someone else cared enough about to put their picture in a magazine.

One day when I got home from GIANT, I stole my way up to the little wooden desk in my room which was tucked away in the alcove below the window that faced the street.

On that window was a Tot Finder sticker that refused to peel away or become unstuck, a reminder for many years after, that not only was the tot who slept in that room long gone, but that I was the very poor parent I knew myself to be, unable to successfully place one on my own children's window some thirty years later, the sticker having peeled off within days, and fallen to the floor under the shades, unstuck and forgotten, no tots likely to ever be found in their room.

At that desk I crafted my letter to Parker Stevenson, pouring out my great desire to perform, to be an actor as he was, asking him what secrets he might impart, and what advice he might suggest for the desperate, young hopeful on the other side of the pencil.

I wrote and re-wrote that letter, honing my language, and trying to imbue the message with the sense that he alone could make a difference in my life, and that I believed in his ability to show me the way, just as I believed he could come to believe in me and my ability to follow the path he would surely outline for me.

The two of us had something special. I was sure of it, and if he didn't somehow know that already, he certainly would after digesting my heartfelt missive.

Copied, and recopied, I lovingly escorted the hand addressed letter to the mailbox at the bottom of Brookfield Road, and then I waited for my response.

To say I believed that this letter represented some kind of Golden Ticket would be accurate. I was caught up in the throes of a fantasy. But to say I was disappointed that I never heard back from Parker Stevenson or saw my letter in print, would not be equally as accurate.

I didn't truly expect anything to happen. I just wanted it to, and wanting something to happen is a lot different than doing anything possible to make it so.

Say for example taking an actual acting class, seeking an agent, or asking my parents to drive me to auditions, something people who want to perform generally engage in.

But again, this was less about being able to perform, something I truly had little interest in, than about being someone I was not, someone who is loved by the masses and receives ongoing affirmation that this love is real, and celebratory, because of who, and what, you are.

Something we can achieve, at least a version of it anyway, when someone crushes on us with the same intensity we are crushing on them.

Which brings us back to Parker Stevenson and my sort of crush, sort of something, though whatever it was, or might have been, it was certainly unrequited, no intensity, no love, no nothing.

It was also something I chased no harder than sending a letter, somehow knowing anything more would be ridiculous.

The question might be whether this lack of returned crushness undermined my ability to crush going forward, the disappointment somehow inhibiting my tweaky crushing energy, ultimately making me more self-conscious about what we can expect when we fall for someone, yet expect nothing in return?

It did not.

I crushed hard after that, and I still do, still obsessing, and still hoping that these obsessions will bear fruit, yet knowing that crushes come and go, and if one doesn't pay off in any kind of satisfying fashion, than the one after that might.

And yet, I still don't quite expect that things will just happen for me, that hasn't changed, and that may be healthy, pragmatic even, just like my perception of Parker Stevenson himself all those years ago.

Which is to say, that maybe I learned something from him after all.

Because in the same way I failed to chase Parker Stevenson, or the idea that he represented a path, is a kind of failure I now know all too well.

And what kind of failure is that?

It is the kind of failure which recognizes that I won't do absolutely anything to get something I want so badly, which is to be a successful novelist, or maybe somehow write for television or the movies.

I won't uproot my family and move to Los Angeles or Brooklyn without a concrete opportunity being handed to me, even though there may be opportunities in those places that Chicago doesn't possess, because it feels unfair to everyone when I can't actually grasp what those opportunities may be.

I won't stop working full-time to write, because then I would compromise my health insurance and retirement plans.

I won't ignore my wife or kids or disappear for days at a time just so I can get more done, because I don't want to be that kind of husband and father.

And so, even though I am insanely jealous of those who can do some or even any of this, I am forced to wrestle with knowing that this is the kind of failure that never quite allows me to take a leap of faith, while still believing that even if things fall apart, and the pieces have to be picked-up, it will have all been worth it.

I'm not even sure anymore that I really sent that letter to Parker Stevenson, but I want it to be true, because I want, need, to believe, that I took a chance, a restrained chance maybe, but still one where I was willing to at least risk a different kind of failure, that of being rejected.

I want this to be part of my story, because rejection unlike risk is something I have come to embrace, and I have always known I would have to do so if I was going to crush again, or want anything at all.

Because ultimately, being rejected has nothing to with whether I am special or cool or deserving of affirmation, it is a necessity, and the next person might feel differently than the one rejecting me now.

And in that I'm sure Parker would agree.

SKETCHES FROM THE ACCIDENT
(FOR ANDRE DUBUS)

1.

I am fourteen years old. I am not a good skier. And yet there I am facing a nameless closed trail that snakes along a ski path named Devil's Playground. The trail runs through a forest and I know it's closed because there is a row of ski poles blocking the entrance to the path. If you want to ski on this trail you must push by these poles, something you do not have to do when a trail is open.

There is also a sign by the entrance to the trail that says, "closed."

I ski down the trail with my friend Aaron and my inability to turn well, much less with confidence is immediately exposed. There are an endless number of trees to get around and as it is not something I am able to with any ease, I ski real slow, I loop as widely as I can around the trees before me, and I focus on one thing, and one thing only—staying on my feet during each poorly executed turn.

Falling seems inevitable, but I do not fall during the run and flush with success and windburn, I decide to join Aaron for one more run.

We slide off the ski lift and easily part the wall of ski poles blocking our path.

Aaron is off like a shot and immediately out of sight. I begin my lumbering run around the trees, leaning left, then right, breathing hard and feeling anxious.

I fall into a semi-rhythm and hope for the best.

My rental skis give a little with each turn, the clamps that connect the boots to the skis straining as I throw my weight around.

The clerk at the rental shop never tightens my ski clamps as much as he could. He tells me that a guy who falls as much as I do should keep them loose.

"Too tight," he says, "and they'll never pop off when you fall."

"So what," I say, "what difference does that make?"

"You don't want to get tangled up in your skis," he says. "You'll break your leg, man, or worse."

I don't ask him what worse is.

2.

I am getting too close to the tree before me, it looms there, dark and gray, its leafless branches envelope me, blocking out sun and sky.

I bang a hard turn to the left. I am already moving slowly, but the turn is even slower. I watch, as my left ski turns parallel to the tree even as my right ski does not. The right ski is suspended for a moment in the snow, and so am I, the ski pops loose and I am now sliding on just the left ski alone. I try to stay upright and as I do I head straight for the tree. My left leg clears it, but my right leg, which is now aloft does not. I slam thigh first into the trunk.

The tree does not give, and I fall into a heap at its base.

I contemplate whether I should get-up and walk down the hill or just lie there in the snow. I feel so tired suddenly, and I'm so comfortable there, the snow like a brand new mattress.

I lay there taking in the cold air, the silence only occasionally disturbed by a skier flying by on Devil's Playground. I start to doze-off, but realize that Aaron may not know that I failed to finish the run.

"Aaron!"

I start to yell his name, but there is no response.

"Aaron!"

I keep yelling and begin to get cold, shivering violently

and uncontrollably.

My right leg is lifeless and it lies before me like a sack of potatoes.

"Help!"

I scream "help" over and over again, but no one comes.

"Help!"

More time passes. I panic. I wonder if anyone will ever come. The trail is closed, who else would even think to ski down it?

As I begin to doze-off again I find myself surrounded by the bearded and red-jacketed members of the ski patrol. They don't say a word and begin to slide me onto a wooden sled. As they do my right leg begins to spasm. I no longer seem to have any control over the muscles on that leg and I scream in pain.

"His thigh muscles have detached themselves from the bone," I hear someone say. The voice is cold and clinical, the person sounds far away.

Someone gives me a shot at the bottom of the mountain.

The pain slowly starts to recede leaving me with something more akin to a charley horse.

They load me into an ambulance, and I finally drift off to sleep.

3.

I awake in the hospital and I'm not sure what's going on. My parents are standing over me and watching as a doctor shaves my right shin with a disposable razor. He is methodical and quick. He picks up a hand drill and starts drilling through my shin about three inches below my knee. He does not say a word, nor does he waste a single motion. When he works his way through the bone and to the other side of my leg, he slides a thin metal rod through the hole. He pauses for a moment, measures the length of the rod now jutting out of the left side of my leg, and cuts off a section with a pair of wire cutters. The doctor surveys his work and looks pleased. He has yet to say a word.

I find out that I have snapped my femur—or thighbone—in half.

One half of the bone has slipped under the other and they need to pull it back, re-connect the two halves, and allow it to set and heal. They could perform surgery and place a larger rod in the bone that would hold it in place until my femur is healed, but given my age, and concerns about stunting my growth, they have decided to put me in traction.

What they are proposing is attaching a clamp to the rod just inserted into my leg and then connecting the clamp to a series of weights and pulleys that will slowly draw the bone together and hold it in place. The healing process will take three months and I will be on my back in traction the whole time.

I am placed in a bed, which is covered by a metal frame that extends from one end of the bed to the other. My right leg is placed in a sling held aloft by the top of the frame and then connected to a pulley that is attached to the part of the frame that is fastened to the foot of my bed. Every time I move the series of weights and pulleys move with me, allowing for a false, but welcome sense of mobility.

After I am fully secured my parents leave for the night.

My father comes back the next day with exercise equipment in hand. A friend of his has lent him a taut, perfectly straight, coiled metal bar with red handgrips on either end. You grasp the handgrips with each hand and then slowly try to bring them together forming an upside down "u." The bar fights you every step of the way and the resulting resistance builds muscle in the pectorals, triceps and lats.

After a couple of half-hearted practice efforts I try to bend the bar into full upside down "u" mode. As I do the right hand grip flies out of my hand and smacks me in the chin as it straightens out.

Blood sprays across my face and gown and for a moment everything goes black.

When I am able to focus again, my jaw is screaming and my dad looks sick.

A doctor is brought in to patch me up.

No stitches are required.

I have only been in the hospital for twenty-four hours.

4.

I cannot leave my bed or get off my back.

I do not go to the mall, I do not go out to McDonald's and I do not go to the movies. I cannot go to the parties my friends are attending or go to school.

I live in the hospital now and I am no longer a member of the world as I have come to know it.

I am in hospital world, and it is all about constants and sameness.

Every day I am awoken at 7:30am so my temperature and pulse can be taken and every day at 7:45am just as I am falling back to sleep I am given my pills—one for constipation and some aspirin for circulation.

I brush my teeth on the tray that folds out of the table next to my bed and the nurses wash my hair for me every day or so, some times less if they are busy.

At some point mid-morning Donna the cleaning woman comes by. She has long dark hair and wears a lot of blush. She arranges her schedule to be in my room every day at 11:00am so we can watch *Young and Restless* together. We don't talk all that much, but to comment on the inanity of the story lines, the subterfuge of the various characters and the prospects of Victor and Nickie ever being happy together.

Just after lunch my tutor Chuck comes by. He has a thick black beard, a receding hairline and wears an army jacket at all times. He never gives me any assignments to work on, and though at one point he does ask me to read a book of essays by Vietnam veterans, we mostly spend our time together hanging out and talking about hospital life. Chuck is a nice guy and I like him, but I never do any schoolwork and no one seems to notice.

As early afternoon blurs into late afternoon, my friend Arnie stops in for a visit. He's got a bowl haircut and freckles on his nose. He tells me about what's going on at school, who's hooking-up with who and what's been happening at the parties I've been missing.

"So, Steve and Sue are going at it in the front yard of Tonya's house, right, and he tries to get down her pants," Arnie says.

"Yeah," I say, "and then what?"

"She says she doesn't go to third with a guy unless she's going out with him," he says.

"All right," I say, "I can dig it, so then what?"

"Steve says, well, do you want to go out with me then?"

"Yeah?" I say.

"And Sue's like okay," Arnie says.

"Cool," I say, "and?"

"And what," he says, "he gets to the third with her."

"Just like that," I say.

"Just like that," he says.

"That's beautiful," I say.

"Yes, it is," Arnie says, "yes it is."

5.

Throughout the day, I have to use a bedpan for bowel movements and a plastic bottle to urinate, and while it is not as bad as it sounds, no one rushes to empty them either. On the one hand even this isn't terrible, because I quickly adjust to the smell.

Hospitals are filled with smells, urine of course, and bowels, but hand creams, salves, soaps, and cleaning products as well.

Soon enough it's all one smell, hospital smell, and part of the background, like white noise.

On the other hand, I eventually have to use the bedpan and bottle again, and when that happens I have a problem. For the most part, the nurses somehow always make it back before there is an accident, but I wait and I wonder, and on occasion I weigh just how much room really remains in the bedpan or bottle lying before me.

On this day, as my calls are ignored and the hours drone on I am forced to urinate into a handful of toilet paper. This is much messier then I expect it to be and as the toilet paper starts to shred and meld itself to my hand I throw it against the wall in a fit of frustration. When the nurse finally comes in I point to the overflowing bottle and the toilet paper on the wall. He takes both without saying a word.

As evening sets-in, my mom comes by to hang out with me.

She has long dark hair which she pulls back with a beret, and she brings me Chinese food from the House of Yu—Won Ton soup, spare ribs, sweet and sour pork, egg rolls—and bags of Haribo gummy Coke bottles.

Except for *Upstairs/Downstairs* my mother never watches television in the real world, but the hospital world is a different and parallel one, and here she watches *Hill Street Blues* with me on Thursday nights, North Carolina State's improbable run to the NCAA title and maybe most important the *Thornbirds* mini-series with its illicit, yet tantalizing love affair between Richard Chamberlain's wayward priest and Rachel Ward, his sexy, but married paramour.

My mom has to leave at some point, and when she does I have to face the biggest obstacle of the day, trying to fall asleep.

I've never slept well anyway, and after the visitors have all gone, the street noise has dissipated, and the hustle and bustle of the hospital has slowed down to crawl, it's just me and my bed, my television and my books

Soon enough, there is nothing to watch, and eventually I don't want to read any more either. At this point I can turn off the light, I can masturbate and I can listen to *The Wall* on my Walkman, but that doesn't mean I will sleep. Having been in bed all-day to begin with, I'm both rested and wired. It might be different if I could move around and find a comfortable position, but I am in traction, which means no squirming, no adjustments and no real movement of any kind.

I am on my back and I will stay on my back, tonight, tomorrow and every day until I leave.

And so it goes most of the time, though tonight I am offered a break from the monotony. They bring in a loud guy with greasy hair and a day's growth. He's been in a car accident and he's accompanied by not only a doctor, but by a police officer as well.

The cop asks him what he's been drinking and the guy says "motor oil." The cop looks at him quizzically and replies in-kind "motor oil?" "Yeah," he says.

The doctor and the cop leave the room muttering to themselves and the guy looks over at me and says "can you believe they fell for that shit?"

A nurse comes in moments later.

"Do you give back rubs?" the guy asks her.

"I do," she says.

"Do you rub anything else?" he asks.

The nurse leaves without saying a word and the guy starts to laugh.

He then looks over at me again and says, "I thought it was worth a try."

I sleep like a baby that night.

He's gone the next day.

6.

Before I entered the hospital I ran like the wind, endlessly flying up and down the hills around my home.

I took flight out there, and could run forever, effortlessly and breathlessly, with wings on my heels and a never-ending reserve of stamina at my disposal.

When my mind wanders here in the hospital I fantasize about running again and it never occurs to me that it won't be the same when I leave.

No one has told me otherwise, and so it's my belief that the day I get out of traction, I will be healed and as good as new, ready to run again.

They don't tell me though that the tendons in my right knee have shrunk from lack of use, or that as strong and mobile as I might feel after three months in traction, my leg can still snap at any time when I first get out.

Nor do they tell me just how much the muscles on my legs have atrophied, or that the blood has barely been circulating through my feet because I have been horizontal and not vertical all this time.

They also don't tell me that when the clamp is taken off and the pin is removed from my leg I will only be able to bend my knee a few degrees, and that when I try to stand for the first time the blood suddenly rushing to my feet will make it feel like I have been hit with a sledgehammer.

And they definitely don't tell me that after three months in traction I will need to re-learn how to walk and that using crutches will leave me breathless and exhausted after merely cruising back and forth down the hall outside my hospital room.

It may be that someone was supposed to tell me all this sooner and forgot, or maybe they just want to protect me. It may also be that people just assume I ought to know all this. It is never quite clear to me. Then again, I learn it all soon enough. I also learn that it's not forever.

After no time, I feel stronger, no longer so exhausted and easily move from two crutches to one.

I walk again too, slowly, and tentatively at first, but I do walk.

My feet stop hurting as well, and though my right knee will be perpetually prone to soreness and pain after this, it does bend again.

One night just months after I leave the hospital, I try to go for a run, though just to the corner and back.

It's dark and cool out, damp, and kind of beautiful, stars everywhere in the clear night sky.

At first I awkwardly plod along and within minutes I'm sweating profusely. Soon I am lumbering from one step to the next, practically dragging my right leg behind me.

I'm not swift or graceful and will not be for months.

It takes me forever to get to the corner and back, but I do it, and I keep doing it, and somewhere along the way as I learn to run again, the path, the crash and even my time in the hospital, all slowly become memories of sometime in the past, all parts of an event I participated in long ago.

FLIGHT TO L.A.

"El-P, who's that?"

My friend Jennifer is over. She's searching through our CDs and looking for songs to download to her iPod.

This is before Spotify and so while sifting through pages of CDs is not as inherently riveting as flipping through vinyl in some dusty store like the one Annie Potts owned in *Pretty in Pink*, it's a long way from not making any effort at all.

The effort still involves a modicum of search and by extension the thrill of discovery that comes by stumbling into something you didn't know was there because you weren't looking for it in the first place.

"The Cars," she shouts excitedly, "you have stuff by The Cars."

Of course I do.

My then four-year old son Myles is quietly watching from across the room. He is entertained by our compulsions, the passion that accompanies the search and the joy we both have when Jennifer sees something she likes.

He is also entertained by watching adults look like kids when we so often have to act like adults around him.

"Oh, what about X?" Jennifer says quizzically sliding out *Los Angeles* and showing it to me.

"Fuck yes," I mouth quietly.

"Noooooooooooooooooooo," Myles who loves X screams springing to action and running across the room.

"No X."

And then he takes the X CD out of her hands.

I am on a plane, I am thirteen-years old, the same age Myles is now and I am flying to Los Angeles, where I am spending the summer with my friend Ricky and his family.

As it is the early 1980's, people are chain-smoking the entire flight. They also serve meals, and not just pretzels or peanuts, but actual meals, and there are actual choices like at a wedding—steak or chicken, even fish. When you are a kid they sometimes even give you leftovers, and when you are traveling by yourself, they definitely do.

Just months before this, I had celebrated my thirteenth birthday with a big party. Not a Bar Mitzvah per se, but definitely a celebration.

My mother had wanted me to dress-up, and I had wanted marzipan on the cake.

We both got we wanted.

My mom had the caterer make marzipan decorations, and I went to the Oakdale Mall with her to shop for my clothes.

Oakdale Mall was home to Aladdin's Castle the arcade we went to before going into the movies, and every other chance we had. It was a cacophony of flashing lights, beeps and whirrs, car sounds and teen angst, and home to Centipede, Galaga, PAC-Man, Pole Position and any other game we now look back on with nostalgia for a decade that everyone claimed they hated when we actually lived in it.

The mall was also home to Hickory Farms where one could buy fancy packaged cheese and sausage long before artisanal shops made this a necessity in places like Brooklyn; GNC, where I bought unwieldy containers of bright orange muscle-building powder that I mixed in with orange juice before school; Anderson-Little, where we shopped for button down Oxfords at the start of the school year; and Fowlers, which passed for a slightly up-scale department store, and where we went that day to buy the dressier clothes I would wear to my party.

We bought navy blue slacks; a powder blue dress shirt; a cream-colored blazer comprised of subtle interlocking grids of blue, brown and gray; and a pair of chocolate brown Docksiders.

Along with my ever-present gold chain and Scott Baio feathered haircut I was ready to become a man, or at least eat marzipan and middle-eastern food with my family and friends.

Shortly thereafter, I was also ready to board my flight to L.A.

I was spending the summer away from my family and upstate New York hometown.

I was heading to the beach, the Santa Monica Pier of *Three's Company* opening credits fame, and all things West—sun, waves, skateboards, palm trees, girls, hopefully, and Hollywood—and my understanding was that people dressed-up for flights in the same way they did for the theater.

It was proper, classy and how things were done.

So I put on my blazer, powder blue dress shirt, slacks and Docksiders and I boarded the plane.

When I stepped off of the plane, the sun beamed down so intensely that the color of the air was a hazy drip of Creamsicle orange and the ground beneath my feet was bleached and filtered through a lens of oozy Marshmallow Fluff.

The rotating Theme Building restaurant at LAX was still in use then, and its flying saucer on legs design promised a mix of adventure and weirdness.

It also seemed to say that the future awaited me, whatever that might be.

"Is that how you dress now?" Ricky asked me in dismay.

He was wearing a faded orange OP surf shirt, long brown corduroy shorts and black and white checkerboard Vans.

I was dressed for Sweeney Todd.

I quickly ditched the clothes, found the beach—and a girl—and discovered both Carrie by Stephen King on sale for 25 cents at a garage sale and Catcher in the Rye by J.D. Salinger buried on a shelf in Ricky's den.

I also found west coast punk—Black Flag, Germs and X, among others.

Well, sort of anyway.

One day I am sifting through the CDs in the punk section at the one-time Tower Records near my office on Wabash below the "L" Tracks. I am new to punk. When people who are my age and who still love punk started loving punk, I was more focused on varsity sports, fitting in and the Doors; followed by inhaling copious amounts of hallucinogens, the Grateful Dead and long, spacey jams. But something had shifted. A desire for noise and punches to the head, vibrating walls and speed, sparse, quick songs that slam and joke, dart into the room and then out again, as the music heads onto the next thing and the next thing and thing after that. No pause, just one musical blow after another is now my thing, and I am consuming all the punk I can, including the band I stumble onto that day, Be Your Own Pet. They are young and angry and funny and fast and I spend the rest of the afternoon listening to their self-titled debut album with equal parts joy, and confusion—how didn't this sound appeal to me when I was their age, and why does it now?

One day as Ricky and I and whoever else we were with knocked around Venice Beach and its menagerie of roller skaters, Vietnam vets, stoners, surfers, Trustafarians, skin heads, homeless and freaks, someone suggested we see *The Decline of Western Civilization* by Penelope Spheeris, the documentary on L.A.'s punk scene in the early 1980's.

It was a scene—the bands, the personalities, the clothes and of course the music—I was not wholly familiar with.

I had been introduced to the Ramones by Adam another friend of ours earlier that year.

The three of us had read the *X-Men* and the *John Carter: Warlord of Mars* books together.

Adam had introduced me to both *The Basketball Diaries* the previous summer, which I had already read at least a dozen times since, and *The Rocky Horror Picture Show* that past winter, repeatedly shouting "virgin" at me as the lights went down.

His opinion was gold.

But the Ramones didn't work for me. I didn't like the speed and the noise—*I Wanna Be Sedated*, maybe, slightly, but the rest of it, I didn't get it. It wasn't The Doors. There was no trippy, banging *Love Her Madly* to be found anywhere—and I dismissed it out of hand.

Now here we were in L.A. during the summer of 1981, watching *The Decline of Western Civilization* and again, I didn't get it, except in this case, it was West coast punk, and I really didn't get that.

Why did anyone like this?

Black Flag?

Loud and stupid.

But what was it, why this visceral response?

Was it just because it wasn't pop or rock enough?

Definitely, maybe.

Was it a class thing, with all the singers seeming so skuzzy to me?

Yes, maybe, Darby Crash definitely did not speak to me.

Maybe it was because I was not in touch with my anger then, and things were not broken enough for me, or more accurately, whether things were broken or not, I wasn't going to let myself feel them regardless?

Yes, most definitely that.

Punk was a reality check, and I didn't need that, and I couldn't handle that, I needed to escape.

More so, I was trying to be something different than all of that, something cool, and popular, someone who finally fit in, felt popular and hooked-up with cheerleaders. I hadn't been able to invite a single girl to my 13th birthday party, and not by choice, or because I didn't want girls there, they just didn't exist for me yet, not until this summer anyway, and I didn't want that any more.

And punk was definitely not the way to get any of that, not in my head anyway.

Which might also mean that this might also be the end of this particular origin story, or whatever this is, I was thirteen, and the things I loved—the X-Men and *Blade Runner*—I loved, and the things I didn't, I didn't, and so much of who we are during those formative years stays formed. We may waver, and wonder about that which we love, a love of all things X-Men and science fiction was no way to be popular then either, and I dropped them for awhile, but I love those things again now, and as fiercely as I did at thirteen.

Punk just wasn't part of all that. But that changed, all of it.

—

A dozen years later I walk-into the Artful Dodger Pub on the North Side of Chicago with my soon to be wife and some friends, we get drinks and head towards the dance floor in the back.

People are dancing, happy, but nothing amazing or especially earth shattering is afoot.

And then there is an explosion.

Not literally, not exactly, but the first beats of *Sabotage* by the Beastie Boys come on, and the joy in the room is suddenly palpable and boundless, people pogoing, arms aloft, smiles wide, heads bobbing, the masses in both perpetual and slow motion all at once, wrapped as they are in strobe lights that are bouncing off of the walls, the ceiling—bending and morphing with them, the beats and all that fucking joy.

I wade into the morass and I never quite come out again.

I have been to the Beat Kitchen in Chicago for readings and fundraisers, once even seeing Alex Kotlowitz read from *There Are No Children Here*, as he sat on a stool on stage drinking a beer, a single light illuminating him—a sight that seemed just ridiculously cool at the time. One night though, I accompany my brother and my quite pregnant sister-in-law to see Avail, a Northern Virginia punk band whose members she went to high school with and has loosely followed around ever since. This is her crowd, thirty-something one-time furious punks, who now have jobs and marriages and children, and who are holding onto what may have been the best part of adolescence—the punk bands that made everything slightly more okay and bearable. I on the other hand am not familiar with Avail in the slightest and I am feeling overly paternal towards my sister-in-law and her still unborn son, as I worry about the loudness that is sure to warp his developing brain and the inevitable mosh pit we will not be able to escape. But then the first chords of *Armchair* come on, the crowd explodes, the band doesn't stop moving or sweating for the next 90 minutes and I am transported above the room, lost in my own developing brain, head cranking, my still to come nephew and worries lost to me, and aware, if only briefly that it doesn't matter who I am, or was, and who is here around me. What matters is being happy, which I am, and it is wonderful.

I suppose at this point it is unnecessary to point out that for most of my life I have been the least punk person I, or you, can imagine, with my compulsive need for 9-5 jobs, my long-running obsessions with health insurance, 401(k)s, a stable home and marriage, structure and steady paychecks.

But *Sabotage*, and Be Your Own Pet, then Avail changed all of that.

I had been dismissive of the Beastie Boys and their idiotic misogyny in high school. But high school was a long time ago, and after listening to Paul's Boutique, and having my brain further flummoxed, I began to wonder that if I was wrong about them, what else was I wrong about?

As it turns out, the Ramones, totally, the speed and the banging songs now spoke to me.

What once seemed like noise was now thrilling, and inspirational.

I wanted to be a writer, and I wanted my writing to sound and look like this, lean and slamming, a punch to the head accompanied by a laugh.

If I was wrong about the Ramones, who else was I wrong about, Minor Threat for one, wow, fuck.

And if I was wrong about them, well, what else, everything maybe, and so I kept searching, and in doing so, I went way back to *The Decline of Western Civilization*, and okay, maybe Black Flag wasn't, and isn't, going to work me even now, but X, yes, that is love, and why was this?

Again there was the speed; the country vibe; the biting lyrics, the aggression—angry, but controlled, and to be honest, I might have control issues, always did, who knew, not me apparently—but there is also the fact that I'm not longer quite so mellow when it comes to the state of the universe.

It started with the Bush administration, and Iraq, but there are the banks, guns, racism, misogyny, poverty, and so much violence, towards so many people, and I feel it all so intensely now. The world is a fucking mess, and I hate it, and how it makes me feel, and yet, expressing those feelings, and feeling those feelings, can come with some humor, and even a kiss, because there is love too, always love. And in that way, I have become punk, still arguably the least punk person you know, but angry, and impassioned, and wanting to articulate it.

I'm open to all of the possibilities anyway, and maybe back then, wandering Venice Beach, wanting to get laid, and be cool, I wasn't open to any of it, couldn't be, everything was too suppressed, and I wanted it all contained.

But not now, fuck all of that, I'm angry and I'm fan boy, and I want to feel it, which is what punk is to me— feeling something and expressing it, no matter how angry and exposed doing so makes you feel—it just took me until my forties to feel any of that.

Which is why despite Myles protestations and his onetime love all things X, I let my friend Jennifer borrow my X CD.

I want her to hear *The World's A Mess; It's In My Kiss*, I want her to feel what I feel, and maybe even what Myles already feels, and knows, hope, anger, joy and speed, and the need to not be so fucking shut-off to the world around us.

I want her to be punk, or at least better understand all of the possibilities she's been missing until now.

GIRLS, GIRLS, GIRLS

I was not one of those kids who kept a journal or diary. I drank. I got high. I ran track and cross-country. I wrestled.

I thought of myself as laid back. I believed I was cool. I kept my emotions under wraps and I liked it that way. I constantly told myself, and anyone who would listen, that nothing bothered me.

I was a senior in high school when I took a required creative writing course. There were some assignments, but mainly we were required to write in our journals as often as possible.

We could write in any style about anything, we just had to write.

I had never written before, or even thought about writing, but I apparently had more than enough material as

I wrote about running and suicide, repeatedly—something that was celebrated by my teacher and her colleagues, and not apparently the cause for alarm in the 1980's it might be today—and my dislike for squirrels, old people and selling raffle tickets.

Mainly though, I wrote about feeling lonely and confused, about love and girls, and more specifically my confusion about my love for one girl: Mary

"My life is weird. Things seem real strange these days. But why? What is causing this chaos in my psyche? Last night I placed this long distance call to Connecticut. I was so happy when I got through and Mary answered. Why can't someone in Binghamton bring this satisfaction to my life? I don't know what it is and I'm really just babbling. My mind's full of jumbled thoughts. You don't even care do you? Do you have any interest in my ramblings? Does anyone? I think Mary does."

In fact I was so sure Mary cared, I wrote an epic poem about her, because I think we all know that epic poems are best suited to capture the drama of having a six-day summer romance with someone one meets at running camp before being torn apart by distance and the start of school.

Did I mention Mary and I met at running camp?

Super cool, right?

And this was 1985 by the way, and so way before *American Pie.*

"The Wind Screams Mary

It's in the papers, it's in the news — And people discuss it over their morning coffee. But I remain fairly oblivious — ignorant to what's going on

The riots in South Africa continue — as the Apartheid issue becomes most frightening — my mom mentioned it once I think

There are people starving to death in Ethiopia — their children being born into a world no one should be — I caught some of Live Aid

People attack Greenpeace unmercifully — an organization just trying to save the world — there was a special report in Sports Illustrated, I skimmed it

Farmers are being ripped-off — the staple of our once great nation — I was forced to see Places in the Heart

And there are murder, suicides, and drug problems, not to mention earthquakes and missing children

But the world's problems float by me — like the errant winds

And why — because I can't be with Mary — and she occupies all my thoughts

Am I selfish — do I have some sort of duty — that I don't know, but I do know that I am but one person and I'm lonely and confused…"

I might add here, that none of this is true.

No one made me see *Places in the Heart*—and I still haven't—and I really did care about most of these things, and read about them, gladly, and on my own.

I clearly thought I needed to sound that way, however, and I suppose a desperate epic poem full of ache and need, couldn't be written any other way.

But I should also ask, again, was I actually in love?

Because while I *thought* that I *thought* about Mary all of the time, Mary may not have been the only girl I *thought* I was in love with. And while long distance relationships are great and romantic in theory, Mary was not where I was. Not like Sarah for example, who I had known for a long time at that point, and who I may have stalked into a friendship—stalking apparently did not have the same kind of stigma then it quite appropriately does now—but who did become an *actual* friend and confidant. Sarah was a girl I trusted and who listened to me when I showed-up at her house late at night to hang out.

"It's not obsession and really not even infatuation. I'm not really sure what it is, it changes as often as night turns to day. You see it's this girl, but she's not just any girl, she is one of my best friends. The problem though, if it actually is a problem and I guess it isn't, hits me that she would be such a quality girlfriend. We've been friends since sixth grade and I can say I know her better than anyone and vice-versa. [Even though] we weren't always great friends, slowly but surely we got close.

We started running together on the off seasons, hanging-out at parties and just having great conversations. I can talk to her, like no one. Anything, any subject, it's awesome. The possible problem though is how could I ruin this wonderful relationship?"

And so, despite my great desire for connection, I actually got more confused when I got close to someone.

Of course, this is may have been a fear of rejection as well, because being rejected by Sarah would have left me where exactly?

Nowhere, that's where.

Mary though, she hadn't rejected me, not yet anyway, and I had not forgotten about her.

"I don't know if what I've been doing is good or bad. Here's the thing. I'll admit I'm probably in love with [Mary], but I'm not obsessed. I'd love to be with her, but I'm not dying. The thing is that I write like I am. You get the impression I'm losing it mentally. So, here's the problem, why do I write like I am dying? Is that what I expect people to think I feel like? Or do I think I should feel like that? There's many questions, but I'm really not sure why I do what I do. Fabricating these obsessive entries. Of course, isn't stuff like that done all of the time? You're with some girl who really likes you, is very good to you, but you don't really like her and since you know that, you can't figure out why you're staying with her. You just do it. There's many such cases, of course they may just be Ben cases, if so you don't have to think about it. By the way, I'm

seeing Mary Sunday, watch out."

I was 17 and I was not merely writing about the human condition, but I was quite sure that all things human condition were only happening to me.

But that's what all teenagers believe, right?

Or was that just me?

Meanwhile, I apparently went to Connecticut to see Mary.

And what did I write about that?

Nothing.

Nothing about the trip there or what I may have been feeling, nothing about going to beach, and nothing about sitting in Mary's parents' car as she and I listened to So True by Spandau Ballet – our song at running camp – and made out, not a single word.

In fact, I never mentioned Mary in my journal again, suddenly, she was gone after all of that and I moved onto another *friend*.

"There's this girl, I think names are basically unimportant, and we've been friends quite awhile (no it's not Sarah, she's another story and world entirely). We became buds when she was in seventh and I was in eighth. She was so cute, she still is, but I'll always remember her like that. I used to call her my little sister, because I couldn't imagine her in any other role. She's written me letters from dance camp – apparently it was all

about camp in the 1980's — and I'd write back. I liked her as a friend a lot. We kind of fell out of whack for a few years (pretty sad, huh?). Well one day last year we were talking like we always seemed to do, just talk about the obvious things, and all of a sudden she said, 'we haven't been really good friends for awhile, have we?' I knew I could count on her to say something like that. Then this year we started to get together and I noticed how really different she was. Not the little girl of my memories, but a real mature, attractive one. We've become really good friends again, but it's really way different. It's cool though, because I'm so comfortable with her, so many ask us if we're dating. We don't, and probably never will, but who really cares. I don't know, I guess I'm mentioning this is because, Saturday night we ended-up going to this party together and everyone else basically paired-up so we were left. We had this great talk. The best we'd ever had. Things are so different from the old days, but I'll tell you, Saturday night I could have fallen in love with her. No doubt in my mind."

And where did that go?

Nowhere.

It is at this time that I might have realized that I might have had a pattern of sorts—falling in love with girls who were friends, and even if those relationships were going nowhere, I didn't plan to try and make it otherwise.

But I didn't realize that, or at least I didn't write about it in my journal.

I might also mention that at that point I was hooking-up

with different girls nearly every weekend, and that I was in fact living a parallel life—craving contact, and in fact having it *physically*, yet still feeling like I was missing something.

But, I didn't write about that either.

And yet, despite the confusion, the yearning and the inability to find love, not all of this was for naught. The class did represent a shift in consciousness for me. Writing in this journal was not only the first time I expressed anything I was feeling, anywhere, but the first time I didn't have to try and convince myself that I was laid back or focus on keeping-up appearances.

Suddenly I could say what I was actually thinking, mostly, and suddenly I had a place to go where I could be inquisitive and confused, and acknowledge that I didn't always need to devalue all of this in an effort to prove to myself that I was cool.

Ultimately, writing in the journal, wasn't even really about love or contact or girls, though it was about all of that too.

I yearned to be heard, by someone, anyone, and in that journal, and on those pages, I was, even if it was only by an audience of one—my writing teacher, Ms. K.

Ms. K. was single and youngish. She had blonde hair, funky teeth and wore short denim skirts.

She was rumored to have slept with the best looking guy from the senior class before ours, which rumors aside, and not unlike suicidal ideation, was not something that anyone seemed especially concerned about in the 1980's.

Or maybe that was just my hometown?

Regardless, we were never able to confirm this sleeping with hot dude one way or another, but we wondered, we always wondered, and this wonder manifested itself in my writing.

For example, one day, I wrote an entry just for Ms. K. when she missed class.

I think I thought I was being funny.

"Ms. K. where can you be? As I sit here mired in depression, fleeting thoughts dart through my mind. Did her Aunt die? Some other relative? Maybe her dog? No I say, death isn't the cause for her absence. Too morbid. It's something else, but what? Once again I start grabbing thoughts. Maybe she reconciled with her boyfriend? Yes maybe she's sleeping in for the day or not necessarily with her boyfriend but some young buck she met at Oscar's or Uncle Tony's? That would be ok, everyone should skip school for that every once in awhile. But then again I don't think its sex she's too old for that... Maybe she's depressed? Good possibility, she is a human being. [But] over what I don't know. Maybe she's over-eating or drinking or BOTH? Maybe she could just be sitting there listening to Lionel Ritchie bumming out?"

Her response?

"Give me a break. No slut here."

The fact is, like all of those girls back then, I thought about Ms. K, a lot.

The difference was that I didn't usually write about her, but I always I wrote to her, and unlike those other girls, she always listened, and she always responded.

Ms. K. heard me at a time when I really wanted to be heard and the proof is on these pages.

I might also add here, that a seed was planted on those pages, though this is only clear to me now in retrospect and so many years removed from that time and place.

Because I wasn't merely heard—not that being heard wouldn't have been enough—I also received attention for my writing during this time period—the endlessly supportive feedback from Ms. K. and the positive comments from other English teachers in study hall who heard about things I had written—like little I had experienced before.

There had been some attention for my running, even my wrestling—less so for my binge-drinking, reading and masturbatory habits—but breaking my leg had pretty much put an end to all of that.

I didn't register what all of that attention meant to me at the time, but it wasn't so long after this when I started to think about writing as I had once thought about running—as an activity that I could maybe do.

That reasons for why I didn't really get started for another 12 years is for another story, and another time, not that the reasons for any of this—not the desire to start, much less all the reasons I could not—became even remotely clear to me for years, but there is this—I was heard, I was somewhat celebrated for what I was doing and I was briefly liberated from my anxieties about almost everything, in much the same ways I was with running before all of that.

I just didn't know it yet.

BELIEVE

The public record does not reflect that two historically significant events occurred in the spring/summer of 1986.

First, I lost my virginity at a friend's house during my second attempt at doing so. The first attempt had been less than successful, the lack of belief in my ability to perform dooming the whole operation to failure before it ever began.

Second, and shortly thereafter, while at the Vestal Drive-in, in a similarly compromising position in the back of my parent's blue station wagon, I took a moment to look out the window and I saw a UFO.

The facts of these events have always been beyond dispute as far as I'm concerned, but there has been no official recognition of either event until now.

Why is this?

In terms of my virginity, and loss thereof, it is my understanding that there is no officially sanctioned body tasked by law with tracking the sexual exploits of teenage boys. Not that the government has admitted to anyway. And certainly not since John Hughes died.

However, regarding my UFO, and yes it is mine, while I'm certain that there is a top-secret agency somewhere that is quite aware of every UFO sighting everywhere, even mine, I am also certain that the sweaty, nearsighted analyst who knows about my presence at the Vestal Drive-in on that night is not allowed to officially report on the details of the evening.

But I am.

I imagine that sex and UFOs, and by extension, sex and space, and by further extension, sex and what we now think of as Nerd culture, are rarely considered in the same breath, much less the same free association, much less conflated to the point where they are intertwined and quasi-dependent on one another.

But hear me out.

Space, like UFO sightings is about infinite possibility, if not an actual rupture of one's consciousness, though the presence of UFOs more specifically represent not just space and the vast unexplored opportunities contained therein, but the possibility that somewhere in the universe there is intelligent life, and someone, or something, beside us which exists, hence ensuring that the chance of us making a connection with someone, or something, is far greater than we could have believed.

By this definition then, sex is of a similar ilk, and yet completely not so at all.

At its best, sex promises at least a moment of connection where none may have previously existed, but unlike space where the possibilities are endless, sex for most, some, is clouded by the lack of opportunity, or the belief that the opportunity to find it is fleeting. Present, then gone, briefly floating there before you like a UFO, ethereal and glowing, and yet just beyond one's reach, unless you, they, us, me, happen to be in the right place, and looking in the right direction, at the right time.

It is luck, and to some extent, available to you because you have been chosen based on some series of calculations you can't quite grasp.

Or, as my mother might say, maybe that's just me.

I am a boy, there is Fat Cat Books and then there is everything else. Fat Cat may technically only occupy a quiet corner in Johnson City, NY, but it dominates the non-school, non-parent, non-everything else free space in my brain. It is where I get my comic books the moment they are released: *The Fantastic Four, The X-Men, The Amazing Spider-Man* and *What If?*. Fat Cat also allows me to imbibe on *The Lord of the Rings* and *John Carter, Warlord of Mars*. And in doing these things Fat Cat allows me to feel normal. If reading science fiction is about escape, then Fat Cat was about escaping to a safe place that allows me that escape in the first place. What am I escaping from? What do you have? Little League, the rich lacrosse-playing kids at camp with their fancy lunches, girls, school, my quasi- anti - Bourgeoisie Jewish intellectual parents who don't fit in and don't care. Pick it, and I want out of it, and away from it, and then somewhere along the way I don't want out of it anymore, I just don't remember now exactly how it all started.

It's important to note, not that it isn't obvious by now, that I was obsessed with space, though more specifically science fiction—it wasn't the stars I cared about, it was the people populating them—long before I was obsessed with sex.

It began with *Star Wars*, but doesn't everything?

And no, you don't need to answer that, I know it does.

To be clear, it's not that my obsession with sex, or even science fiction, starts with *Star Wars* exactly, but the idea of obsession as a thing or a life force, and the feeling of wanting to experience something so badly that you're willing to consume it, and even destroy it, certainly did.

It's about wanting something all of the time.

It's also about not being able to think about anything else.

That was *Star Wars* for me.

It was new and different, and a manifestation of all the things I was already obsessing about, space, escape, heroism, fathers, and I suppose sex as well, even if I didn't quite get that yet.

Close Encounters of the Third Kind would soon grab me in a similar fashion.

It dared me to believe that there was something bigger out there and unexplained, and that whatever it was, was worth chasing, because it spoke to the possibility that maybe things could be explained, and if that was possible, then Little League and rich kids didn't have to have so much power over me, and the world didn't have to be so confusing.

In 2015 all of this is somehow cool. People want to talk about the *X-Men* or *Star Trek*, or at least go to the movies like *Star Wars* so they can talk about them if they have to. But back then—and I don't care how successful *Star Wars* was—that wasn't the case. None of it was cool, and for a moment, that was fine with me.

—

In 1996 I start a new job. It is at a nonprofit and there is a lunch room, the kind of place I've always avoided on previous jobs because going to lunch gets in the way of reading, or wandering the streets, searching for arcades and bookstores and who knows what. But this lunch room is different. In this lunch room there is a white board on the wall and once a week the staff meets to discuss the *X-Files* and slowly map-out the iconography that compromises the show's endless search for the truth. There with the black oil and the cigarette smoking man, Mulder's lost sister, and The Lone Gunmen, the bespectacled freaks I might have in fact been friends with if I had followed the path I was on as a kid. But I hadn't followed that path, not at all, much less spent much time at all on anything science fiction or speculative in years. I haven't even been watching *X-Files* when I start the job. And yet there is something that speaks to me about the show and these discussions about something out there I haven't even quite known existed. I am being invited into this inner sanctum of weekly discussions, speculation and conspiracy-laden diatribes. There is connection, and it is like magic, and while maybe not an entirely conscious thing, it is also the start of a reconsideration of everything I have been running from.

———

During the summer of 1981 *Escape from New York* was released, and I was hanging out in Los Angeles with my friend Ricky and his family. While there, I met Paula, which is quite possibly not her actual name.

Paula was a beach babe with long blondish brown hair and a propensity for cut-off jean shorts and bikini tops. I stared at her for days, but did not speak to her, instead choosing to follow her around like a lost puppy, needy and hungry for attention.

Snake Plissken would have been disgusted.

When we finally spoke, we were on the beach, and I became so erect in my canvas gym shorts, that I could not contain it, much less hide it, and had to roll onto my stomach until it subsided.

Paula and I ran around all summer after that.

She liked me to wear the dress pants and shirt I had brought with me from home and a Puka shell necklace she picked out for me. She also liked me to wear taxi driver caps. All of which I wore for her in different arrangements, at different times, throughout the summer.

The last day I was in Los Angeles she asked me to wear the whole ensemble so I could have my picture taken for her at the Galleria where they would later film scenes for both *Fast Times at Ridgemont High* and *Terminator 2*.

It was brutally hot, and I sweated through the whole

experience. I would have done anything for her though. It was the closest I had ever really been to a real girl.

After the photo was taken Paula cried and said she would write.

We had never even kissed, and we never saw each other again.

In 1982, I went on my first date. It was with Tonya, also likely not her actual name. Tonya was lovely. She had this beautiful, creamy skin, an enormous smile and long hair. We went to see E.T. at the Oakdale Mall in my hometown.

It was our only real date, and while it included an alien and space, the alien was cuddly and mainstream, and while still magical, it coincided with my move away from comic books and science fiction and their place in my universe.

My focus was narrower now, trying to be cool, and hook-up, and my obsessive tendencies had shifted to sex, how to get it, and keep it when I got it, assuming I ever figured any of that out.

Tonya and I made out almost every morning before homeroom under the stairwell by one of the side exits at school. That too was magical until it was over. I broke my leg, spent the winter in the hospital and Tonya broke-up with me as I lay there in traction.

—

The Terminator was released in 1984, but so was *Sixteen Candles*. I watched the former like I had found a new religion—though it was really just the last dregs of my old religion—and yet, it was the latter, with Farmer Ted, drunken seniors, parties and panties that I came to believe could be my destiny.

That winter I was invited to a party following a big win for our high school basketball team. As a runner, and by now a varsity athlete, I was not without access to parties, but not these kinds of parties. Not ones with real athletes, i.e., the basketball and football players, and more importantly, cheerleaders.

I had never spoken to a cheerleader, not a varsity one anyway, or one older than me, hence a real one. I had seen them in the halls—at times mere centimeters away—laughing and full of swish, but that's it, they might as well have been extraterrestrials for all the contact I'd had with them.

That changed when Rhonda, and no, her name wasn't Rhonda—we both know that by now—walked up to me.

Rhonda was from the East side. She had wavy blonde hair and she was chewing gum and she had this smile that was sparkly and transfixing. She was also wearing tight jeans.

She was older than me and cool, really cool. Basically,

she was John Hughes material.

"Are you a friend of Joe?" she asked.

"I am," I said trying not to look incredulous, or weird, or whatever applied.

Joe—his real name because he so wouldn't care if he knew he was showing-up here—was a teammate and friend. He was older, he had great hair, really great hair, maybe the best hair ever, and he served as a mentor of sorts in terms of navigating women, dating and high school.

All of which seemed legit, because chicks really dug him.

"Cool, do you want to go upstairs?" she asked.

Of course.

We found a room.

Rhonda pulled me on top of her.

We were all hair and grind.

I started to obsess.

Was I going to fast or too slow?

Should I take out the condom that was slowly melting in my wallet from lack of use while I still could?

Were we supposed to take off all of our clothes first?

Do I ask about any of this?

"Should I get a condom out?" I finally, and breathlessly, asked looking at her in a panic.

Rhonda pushed me off of her and left the room.

I never spoke to her again.

I spoke to Joe though.

"If you have to ask," he said shaking his head, "you should always assume the answer is no."

I now had something new to obsess over—when to ask and whether you can ever really know when it's time to do so unless the person you're with tells you it is?

What I was not obsessing over was the upcoming release of *Aliens*, or anything really that didn't involve jeans, T-shirts and boobs.

It's 1997 and I am at the rehearsal dinner for a friend's wedding, and as a late addition I am sitting with the distant cousins, and an uncle, who is a successful lawyer, and by all appearances, a normal adult. We talk because we have no one else to talk to, and he asks me what I know about JFK's assassination. Or, more accurately, what I really know, because you know, it didn't go down as we've been led to believe. It involves the government, and the mob, it was a hit, part of a vast conspiracy overseen by shadowing figures who felt Kennedy knew too much, and not just about Cuba, or the mob, but aliens, Area 51 and Roswell, and I know all about that don't I? I do, sort of, but he is happy to tell me all about it anyway. I see his son roll his eyes. He's heard it all before. I keep listening though, because I assume the uncle is happy to have a captive audience, though even more than that, that he is happy that maybe someone, anyone, will believe what he knows to be the truth. And since I did—and do—believe it's all possible, I want to be that person for him.

It is now 1986 and Natalie, so very not her actual name, announced in the school cafeteria that she *would* sleep with me before I graduated from high school. When this information reached me in the way these things do, someone told someone who told someone who told me, I made a beeline for her.

I didn't have to ask anything but, "when and where?"

We agreed to meet at my house the next day after track practice.

It did not go so well.

In retrospect, should I have jerked-off right before she came over in an effort to prevent premature ejaculation?

Maybe not.

But should I have a second time to be safe?

Definitely not.

Still we worked it out just weeks later and then I asked her to go to the drive-in with me.

We were in the back of the station wagon, and I know you are supposed to keep your eyes closed, because that's what Joe told me, and possibly a character played by Molly

Ringwald, but I didn't, and I rarely did. I liked to watch, and as we shifted into some kind of compromising position, the night was so very dark, the moon a million miles away, and, because we didn't go to the actual drive-in, but instead parked behind it, it was so quiet, and there were no distractions, it was just us, only us, and I looked out the window and there it was, a ship of some kind, off above the car, hovering for a moment, glowing and cylindrical. I locked into it, and I looked for any signs that would make it anything but a UFO—numbers, logos, wings or a tail, a cockpit—but there wasn't anything. It was a UFO, which I watched until it moved away, and then I lingered there for a moment, awaiting its return, something, anything, but there was nothing. It was ephemeral, and now it was just me and Natalie again, alone, the two of us, and nothing else.

The next day the newspaper reported the sighting and went on to say that there were no military planes or weather balloons in the area that night.

Not that I can find any reference to that article now.

Regardless, there was no formal explanation for what I saw.

One explanation not reported, however, is that I saw the UFO because I was finally having sex, that is was a manifestation of what was going on for me internally, a break with consciousness and the desperation I felt, which manifested itself in access to not just a new world, but all worlds, the one we live in, the ones out there, parallel worlds, all of them.

All of which would be cool, and may even be true, at least I choose to believe that's a possibility anyway. But I also have to recognize how the UFO appeared to me as my childhood fascination, and obsession, with space, and all things science fiction was fully passing.

The question for me now, is whether I had truly eschewed all of that as a means for fitting-in and getting laid, or had I merely outgrown it?

Was the UFO a message from something larger than me, and what I could actually grasp at the time, thus, maybe not a break with consciousness, but a break with who I had been up until that point, now lost to space and youth?

Also, who the fuck do I think I am asking these questions in the first place, Richard Linklater?

It is 2000 and I am on a new job at another nonprofit, this one focused on child abuse and neglect, and at the last minute I am invited to a marketing meeting with a number of the organization's Vice Presidents and an actor who makes public appearances at children's events as Spider-Man and wants to know whether there is some way we can work together. The actor's appearances are officially sanctioned by Marvel, who doesn't care much at the time what happens with the character. Cash-flow isn't great for them, and while the Spider-Man movies with Toby Maguire are soon to come, there is seemingly no belief that superheroes can expect to receive much attention beyond die-hard fanboys and those who attend Comic-Con. The actor shows up in character and the other members of the staff are flabbergasted. They have no idea what Spider-Man's back story is, much less how to engage him. I am not expected to participate, but being the only person who speaks Spider-Man, we go on to talk about Gwen Stacey's untimely death, the tragic loss of Uncle Ben and the responsibility that comes with having great powers. My co-workers are too stunned to say much and ultimately no one but me sees any value in working with a superhero that popular culture has passed by. After the meeting one Vice President after another walks out shaking their heads and smiling at me, but none of them is smiling bigger, or harder, than I am.

"I never got *Star Wars*," Debbie, so totally the correct name, said the night I met her.

It was 1987 and I had been drawn to her legs and long brown hair, but it was the fates, and our roommates locking the door to my dorm room to have sex, that pushed us together and led to us talking all night about our mutual love for *Days of Our Lives* and *Soap*, the show, not the product, and her inexplicable preference for the clearly second rate, and derivative, *Knot's Landing* over *Dallas*.

Still, while there was connection, and alchemy, Debbie said she didn't get *Star Wars*.

It didn't really mean anything to me at the point, and maybe nothing beside somehow, eventually sleeping with her was all that really did matter. But it had once, and *Dallas* was one thing, but could I be with someone who didn't like *Star Wars*?

Apparently I could and apparently I had crossed over the dark side myself, because later I decided to ask Debbie to marry me.

It was now 1994, and not a great year for science fiction movies at all, except for *Star Trek: Generations*, maybe, which to be honest, I didn't even go to see.

We were driving cross country Debbie and I, and I had been desperately carrying an engagement ring with me for days, hoping for the right moment to propose.

But there wasn't a right moment, or I wasn't ready, or something, and so as we were driving through Wyoming, dodging Bison, and torrential rains, and I committed myself to asking the next day no matter what.

What didn't initially occur to me is that our plan has already been to camp next to Devil's Tower, the location of the climactic finale to *Close Encounters of the Third Kind*.

What could be more perfect?

We pulled into the campsite late at night, it was dark and impossible to see much of anything, much less Devil's Tower itself. However, there was one thing we could see very well, there was a sheet stretched between two trees and they were showing *Close Encounters of the Third Kind*.

Boom.

Magic.

Karma.

Something.

Everything.

"Oh, my God, look," I said to Debbie.

She looks.

"Ughhh, is that *Close Encounters*, I hate that movie," Debbie replied.

Did this cause me pause?

It did.

Of course, I had been pausing for days now.

I was done pausing.

I asked Debbie to marry the next morning at the base of Devil's Tower.

Debbie and I do not talk about *Star Wars* or UFOs, and she never dug *X-Files*, but that's been okay, we've had *The*

Sopranos, bills to pay, trips to Los Angeles, co-workers to complain about and doughnuts to eat.

Two things have changed though, and while not as profound as losing my virginity or seeing a UFO, they have had a significant impact on what I am now, or at least how I live now.

First, the world has caught up with who I once was.

Second, Debbie and I had children who love science fiction and superheroes.

They think it's fascinating that Luke and Leia are actually brother and sister. They want to argue about who would win a fight between The Incredible Hulk and The Thing. They beg me to show them any scenes from Game of Thrones that involve dragons burning cities and tearing people in half.

And with every Marvel movie we go to together, and every time I skip work to watch Mad Max: Fury Road on opening night without them, or binge long into the night watching Orphan Black or Daredevil in a sweaty, joyous frenzy, I have come to recognize everything I gave up to become something else, and that not only can I be what I am now and that other person too, but how much I missed all of it.

I suppressed my desire to be a fanboy because I wanted to be cool.

The fact is though, I want to dissect the storylines of

Game of Thrones at work and understand where and how the show and books deviate. I want to attend the Chicago Comic & Entertainment Expo and pose for pictures with people dressed-up as Spider-Man. And I want to believe that J.J. Abrams is going to get the new *Star Wars* movies right because he has too.

I have come home.

All that's truly missing is a return visit from my UFO.

It will be thirty years this summer since I last saw it, and it hasn't reappeared yet. But I'm ready, and I'm waiting, and I believe.

Again.

SKETCHES FROM THE (OTHER) ACCIDENT

1.

I'm sitting in bed and my back is against the wall.

My stomach is bloated with Chinese food—sweet and sour chicken, Won Ton soup, egg rolls and spare ribs—but I'm not really focused on any of that.

Nor am I exactly focused on my left hand, which is freshly, and heavily, bandaged, and which I'm holding straight up in the air.

And I'm definitely not focused on the accident that has transpired just hours before.

Not really anyway.

Instead I'm staring at my girlfriend who is mostly naked—she is a wearing a T-shirt—on top of me and grinding, eyes closed, head swaying, small bubbles of sweat, popping-up on her brow and upper lip.

And so if I'm focused on anything it is her thighs, ecstasy and the impossibility of it all—the all being how one gets from there to here, and maybe even that I get to have sex with anyone, something that still mystifies me in same way paid vacation time will years later.

But then she moves in some unexpected way, or maybe I do, none of this is totally coherent, my bandaged hand slams into the wall behind me and I spring awake.

2.

The grass is high and wet, the wheels too low, and the mower blade is getting blocked with all the jagged, soggy clippings.

I begin to picture the screaming and the crying that is soon to come, and I wonder yet again what the hell I'm even doing here.

Is this really how I want to spend my days?

Is this how I want to live my life?

How did I even get here?

At this point I don't know what to do or what to think.

It's all just too confusing.

I flip the mower over, and I'm sure I turned it off. Well,

I'm sure I think I did. But who knows at this point, I'm fucking spinning.

The mower doesn't work right.

The on-off switch is fucked, defective, obsolete, whatever, it doesn't work.

I can pull the spark plug, which will kill the engine, but I am not allowed to, it's bad for the engine, and so instead, I have to cover the muffler with my hand until the engine sputters and dies.

Which again, I'm sure I did.

But did I?

And even if I did, engines can sputter back to life, so who knows, I don't, I really don't.

What I do know is that there's the blade and it's rotating, and for just a moment I am mesmerized by the motion, and then there is a clunk, because a moment's distraction is all it really takes.

The heavy blade stops moving.

Then my brain stops.

Then time stops.

And I can suddenly see myself from every direction all at once. I am the only person in the universe, and it's oddly moving, and other-worldly.

But then there is the blood, so much blood, spraying everywhere, and instead of thinking, wow, that's my blood, or even, wow, that's fucked-up, I think, wow, just like the horror movies.

It's all slow motion for a moment, there is me alone, unmoving, and intergalactic, and then blood, everywhere, like the bullets flying in *Matrix*, like someone, me, could reach out and touch it.

But all of that is ruined when my boss suddenly appears and he is screaming.

3.

A friend knows I need to earn some money. He also knows that Terry is looking for some workers to join his landscaping crew.

He introduces us, and from jump Terry seems to offer something different, something enticing, a gingerbread house if you will.

He buys us lunch and offers to get us stoned.

He listens to the Grateful Dead and regales us with stories about the local girls he is banging.

We can come and go as we please just like he does.

On top of all that, he offers to pay us top dollar just to mow lawns.

And so just like that the trap is set—the visions of freedom and money, and the chance, maybe, somehow, for pussy, manifesting itself as a swirling mass of potential awesomeness.

But that is just the vision, or projection, or whatever one should call it.

The reality is long days, with lunch in the truck as we rush from one site to the next and banal stories about young girls and sex that overwhelm with their depravity.

"She's a virgin, a fucking virgin, and I meet her on a job as I'm talking to her mom, and she's so young and soft, and when I fuck her for her first time, she's saying over and over again, 'oh Terry, oh Terry, oh Terry' in this soft voice."

I know this girl, and she is a girl, and picturing this gap-toothed, predatory, motherfucker, with his sloppy gut and sweaty man boobs on top of her, makes me feel ill.

The reality is also a stoned, angry boss screaming and crying at me about how slow I am and my poor technique, and the short length of the grass when I am done—customers may like their grass short, even expect it, but short grass leads to less mowing, and less mowing leads to less drug money.

"Are you trying to fucking put me out of business? Are you trying kill me? I mean Jesus Christ, raise the wheels. Raise the fucking wheels."

I just nod, I know the drill, and I've already raised the wheels.

"And why the fuck is it taking you so long. I can mow twice as fucking fast as you guys."

Terry then proceeds to push one mower in front of

him while he pulls another behind him.

"How hard is that? Jesus. My dad would have fucking killed me if I mowed as slow as you fucking do. Are you even trying?"

More nodding, I can never go fast enough, or mow straight enough, or leave the grass high enough, and it's really kind of pointless to try.

The reality is, the job was not cool or fun and I wonder what happened to that vision? I also wonder how one summer became two, and how I have allowed myself to come back and work for Terry again?

It's true that there is no other work, but this is on me, right?

Soon all I have is the money to think about and ultimately I wonder if I should just quit? Just run off. The problem though is that lately Terry hasn't been paying me regularly. Check that, he has never paid me regularly, but now it's added up to a fairly substantial amount.

So, what am I supposed to do, quit with him owing me money?

Then what?

I'll never get paid.

And so the trap draws tighter.

Now it's not just that I've been sucked in, again, but I can't even fight for my freedom because that freedom comes with a cost.

And with such a cost, does it even qualify as freedom?

Such questions come to dominate my days and nights and there are no answers or end in sight.

4.

The drive to the hospital is a blur.

The cacophony of Terry repeatedly screaming, "Oh, Jesus," replacing the accident in my head and the layer of surreal now enveloping all thoughts related to the day.

I am resting my slashed, but not quite severed fingers tips, on a greasy McDonald's bag in my lap as we fly through the South side of town.

Terry's screams and cries begin to morph and merge into a wave of white noise, a sound machine accompanying a journey that is otherwise calm, and possibly the result of shock, but still, everything has become a wave, the screams, the streets, the fingers, all washing over me, now and forever.

This continues even as we walk into the emergency room, which looks like a war zone—people everywhere, running, crying, and endless range of activity—everything at high speed, but me, I am a buoy, bobbing and stable, as the world wraps around me and passes by.

"What are you doing here? How did you know?"

Someone is talking to me.

Someone I know, but am not friends with.

She seems in awe that I am standing there before her, but why?

I soon realize that she is not the only person I know in the emergency room. I know everyone. It's like a keg party, but the joy and lust has been traded for confusion and fear.

I can smell it now.

Then she looks down at me and she is jolted out of her reverie.

She takes a step back and she starts to scream.

5.

When I was I was a child, and long before the lawn mower accident, or the skiing accident, I had a string of smaller accidents.

I was hit in the head with a baseball bat at school, which did not require stitches, and a hockey stick on the street where I lived, which did.

I tore my hand open at camp one summer sliding down a hill, and there were stitches; and then my head, sliding down the hill in front of my house, more stitches; I slipped climbing a waterfall—a small waterfall—after taking just a step or two passed the sign that said do not proceed further, and ripped open my elbow, stitches, again.

I also jammed a pencil in my face when I was toddler, ran head first into a bench in pre-school, when I could not decide whether to jump over it or dive under, lots of blood, lots of stitches; and I fell into an air conditioner at an airport, sliced my lip, and got, yes, stitches, though they were the dissolving kind.

I can't imagine what my parents went through during all of those years, they never said a word, they were there to pick me-up, to look away, to love me, but never a word about any of it. Of course, they must have decided, unconsciously maybe, though maybe not, that being numb to all, any, of this, was better than actually thinking about it.

My grandmother though pulled me aside one day when we were visiting her, and said, "If you keep having accidents, I will have to stop loving you."

That seemed really fucked-up to me at the time, but I totally get it now.

6.

My dad enters the room I've been sitting in. I am no longer calm or Zen. There is no white noise or waves. There is just my hand which has grown increasingly stiff, the dried blood that is still everywhere—and never will quite leave my boots—and the screams, which are constant.

There had been a party.

People I know.

A bunch of cars heading home.

And a crash.

A friend of mine had been thrown out of a side window—both hips cracked—but they hadn't figured that out yet, hence the never-ending screams as they tried to determine what was going on, all the people I know in the emergency room, and the complete lack of attention I've been receiving. Because it's all hands on deck for this friend, and now there is my father, somber, and horrified, and me, finally freaked-out in my empty, cold room, and wondering if anyone is ever going to help me at all.

Soon my mother arrives as well, and still, we sit.

But then the screams fade and there are nurses and I'm counting backwards from one-hundred and I am in recovery and I'm freezing and they remove a blanket from a pizza oven built into the wall next to me and now I'm toasty and asleep and awake again and being sent home where I eat Chinese food, have sex and slam my newly stitched fingers into the wall behind my bed.

7.

"What are you talking about?" my friend Avi says over the phone.

I'm supposed to meet Avi in Albany that coming weekend for an ultimate Frisbee tournament, but now I cannot play. I'm going, but only to watch, and I'm trying to explain to him why this is.

Avi's not totally hearing me.

"I just saw you last weekend and you were fine," he says incredulously.

And I am fine.

I am not in pain, anyway.

So fine, right, yes, I think so.

8.

I do not have to mow lawns anymore and no one is yelling at me. My fingers remain bandaged, but I otherwise go about my day—running; sort of playing ultimate Frisbee; sort of having sex, never on top certainly; drinking and getting high.

I can't use my left hand for anything, but there are worse things than that.

For example, a couple of weeks later I wake-up and

my fingers feel dead.

What does dead feel like?

I don't know, not exactly.

When I went to bed I felt like I had fingertips, they dynamic and organic, with some movement, and well, life.

Now they don't feel like this, they don't exist, I'm sure of it.

But what do I know?

A lot apparently, because later that day I go to see my hand doctor and he doesn't look very happy.

He is smiling his smile, because he's always smiling, but even as he's smiling he's clearly not happy to see me.

The hand doctor is from Italy and the color of Cappuccino.

And what does that matter?

It doesn't, but that is what I'm focusing on, or trying to anyway, not his smile, or his not happiness.

He grabs my hand forcefully, yet still with a certain gracefulness—it's all dichotomy on this day—and pulls it under a sink.

He removes the bandages that cover my ring finger and pinkie and starts to vigorously scrub them.

As he does the tip of my ring finger melts.

And what does that look like?

I don't know, the cells are all dead and they wash away in the sink.

The tip disappears, or at least the substance of it does.

The hand doctor really stops smiling.

He needs to amputate the tip of my finger. They will replace the skin with a graft from my hip.

I am back in the hospital and I am counting backwards again and after that my finger hurts all of the time and if I bang my hip, it's like being hit with a sledge hammer.

This is what the rest of the summer looks like.

This is what might be called worse, not fine.

I am not fine, and I have no finger tip on my ring finger, just a brand new layer of skin.

I am now all nerve-ending and pain.

9.

One night, later, back at college, drunk and high and laying around in Debbie's dorm room one night, I am no longer in pain and I am staring at the finger.

When the tip was removed, I lost the nail, but the Cappuccino hand doctor said it would grow back.

Now it has, and it is mutant, and warped, like a helmet or shield, curved and slowly covering the amputated tip.

The hand doctor told me this would happen, that it could become a problem if not trimmed back, but I've been scared to do so, all raw flesh and weirdness awaiting me.

But tonight, staring at the nail which I have let grow for far too long, I can't stand looking at it anymore, and can't stand myself for being such a pussy.

I ask Debbie for a nail clipper.

I line it up.

I close my eyes.

And I start to clip away.

MEXICO CITY BLUES

We were in Mexico because of my mother. It was her idea to take my brother Adam and I south of the border.

Her vision was that we would see the great artists of Mexico City—Rivera, Orozco, Siqueras and Kahlo—and then hit the beach in Cancun.

And then she made it so.

Things started going wrong almost immediately though.

I am pick-pocketed outside of our hotel and make the mistake of re-tracing our steps back to the bar we were in by cab, though now it is really dark, and I don't know the language and everything—even stopping for gas—suddenly seems scary.

We attend the bullfights on amateur day and one

bullfighter is so inept that people start cheering for his death, and as we wonder whether we are going to watch him die, a guy next to us leaps out of his seat and kills the bull right in front of us with a knife he is carrying.

We are the Temples of the Sun and the Moon, we are the only tourists there, and after Adam politely says, "Cuanto," to a beggar trying to sell us a wall-hanging, he proceeds to follow us around for the next hour near tears as he desperately tries to close the sale.

But it is on our third night in Mexico, a country where everyone actively discourages one from drinking the water that we make a grave mistake—we all decide to order shrimp scampi.

I can't remember what the meal tastes like; I can tell you however what happens the next day at the airport as we prepare to catch our flight from Mexico City to Cancun and the next phase of our trip.

It starts with Adam saying he had to go to the bathroom.

We wait, and wait, but as the minutes passed it begins to seem less and less likely that he will return, and at some point I go to look for him.

The bathroom is dark and quiet and Adam is nowhere in sight.

I walk up to the row of stalls and call out his name.

"Adam, you still in here?"

"I'm over here," Adam says, his voice quavering and sounding like a junkie looking for his next hit.

"Hey man, what's going on?" I ask as I work my way to his stall.

"I have diarrhea," he replies. "I didn't make it all the way to the toilet."

"Shit," I say, my expletive matching the mood, "are you okay?"

"I need another pair of shorts," he says, "and I need them now. Some guy has been pounding on the door and screaming at me in Spanish."

I run out of the bathroom and sprint to the nearest newsstand. They have no shorts. Nor are there any at the duty-free shop. I wander the terminal; no shorts are to be found.

This is not the airport of today, mini-malls full of Starbucks and Bennetton stores, massage tables and Polo golf shops.

This is pre-globalization, and it is an entirely different time and place.

The first George Bush is in office, MTV actually shows music videos and Barry Bonds is still a string bean hitting no more than 30 homeruns a year for the Pirates.
This airport has the basics—the International Herald Tribune, cheap rum and imported cigars– and that is it.

I walk-up to a young traveler type, one of those guys

you see at every airport. They have one backpack on their back where it belongs and another on their chest, where it does not. They're wearing dirty, faded Columbia shorts and scuffed leather sandals of indiscriminate origin. They have a scruffy, not-quite adult beard and disheveled near Jew-fro hair. Their t-shirt has some obscure reference to Machu Picchu or some island, somewhere, where people drink hallucinogenic tea before dancing all night beneath a full moon.

The guy can be from anywhere, but he tends to be from Australia doing that walkabout thing they do.

"Hey dude, excuse me," I say.

"Yeah mate," he replies.

Bam, called that.

"My brother had some bad shrimp," I say a little pan-icked, "and he didn't quite make it to the bathroom, and now he needs some shorts, and I'm hoping you might be willing to sell me a pair."

I want to be cool, but I am not—I am desperate. If this guy won't help me, we're fucked, it's that simple.

"Sure man, no problem," he says smiling reaching into his bag—the front one—and pulling out some shorts, "you can have them for free."

I want to hug him, but that seems too personal, plus how am I going to get around his front pack, now open and gaping before me?

Still, I want to do or say something.

"You rock brother," I say, "and that Pat Cash, cool dude, handsome too."

"Right," he says turning away, "good luck with everything."

I dash back to the bathroom and pass Adam the shorts under the door. He is gaunt and ragged when he finally comes out, but feels fine by the time we got on the plane.

My mom though can't say the same.

"I'm feeling very sick," she tells me as we take off.

"Let's see if they have some Alka-Seltzer," I say.

"No," she says, "that won't help."

That response is expected.

My parents don't believe that medicine is ever helpful, they won't take anything and for years all we have had kicking around the medicine chest in our house was an ancient, unused bottle of aspirin and a home colonic that no one had ever opened.

I think this has something to do with showing weakness, and an aversion to products and brands, and anything corporate, though mostly they don't like being told what to do, and the act of taking medicine somehow acknowledges that someone, somewhere off behind a curtain is doing just that.

In that moment, I am reminded of another trip, and another time, my dad is on this one, and we are off somewhere in the Everglades when my mother suggests that we try and see a movie.

Broadcast News is playing somewhere, down some series of dirt roads and we are told by the woman at the front desk that we can't possibly get there on time.

That is the wrong thing to say.

My mother is sure we can get there on time.

We all complain that there's no way, that we don't want to miss the beginning of the movie and that there are alligators everywhere.

But my mother gets us all into the car anyway and then after taking a number of left and right turns through the dark swamps—all of this well before there are cell phones and GPS in every car—we get to the theater where the girl at the ticket counter tells us the movie has started.

My mom tells her she doesn't think that's the case, and when we go in, it hasn't.

It's as if she had morphed into Hiro Nakamura and bent time and space to her will because she was told something couldn't be done.

It is part of the family folklore now.

Despite all that, I stop the flight attendant, who brings my mother the Alka-Selzer.

My mother drinks the Alka-Seltzer.

"Wow, that's incredible, it really works," she says.

The Alka-Seltzer incident becomes part of the family

folklore as well and our touchstone for every discussion on the benefits of over-the-counter medicine from that point forward.

After we land I become so sick that, after making myself vomit for an entire afternoon, I am forced to lie in bed for two days.

I watch Mexican soap operas, drink bottled water, and while I should be dreaming of bland foods like white rice and toast, comfort foods—that fact is, we didn't do that either when I was growing-up, we didn't follow rules, we dreamed what we dreamed—I dream of chicken fajitas.

I do get healthy though, and outside of the moment days later when we actually have to question whether or not Adam is dead, the trip really is quite lovely.

I should pause here to say that in terms of the whole dead Adam thing, there is an evening near the end of the trip, where there is a question of whether Adam has drowned while jogging on the beach and the tide comes in, but he does not.

My mother, now healthy herself, sunburned and lovely, her hair still all black and long, is convinced that Adam has died.

"What am I going to tell dad," she says over and over again.

I don't believe Adam has drowned, but when the hotel finally says they will look into sending out a helicopter to search for him I start to wonder as well.

Minutes later when he walks in barefoot and tired after getting lost and being forced to walk back to the hotel along the highway I realize just how terrified I have been.

I also realize that it might be time to go home, which we do, at that point smiling, and full of love, the good memories far outweighing the stolen wallets, murdered bulls, stomach problems and near drownings.

At least that's how I remember it. Memory is a funny thing though, and I wonder if Adam remembers the trip the same way I do.

I email him the draft of this piece and ask him for his thoughts.

He replies immediately.

Dear Ben,

Your memory of the story is actually a bit more sanitary, pardon the pun, than what I remember. My memory of this story is that you, Mom and I went to the airport and we divided up the jobs. You had to do one job, mom had to do a second job and the third job was that I was going to wait in line for all of us to check in.

Quite a long line in a hot and crowded airport, I might add. As I was waiting in line recognizing that I was doing a job that would not only affect my travels but yours and mom's as well, I felt quite nauseous and a strong sense that I had to use the bathroom. I said to myself that for me to get out of line and then for you and mom to come back from your jobs and for us to have started at the back of the line again was just not acceptable. We might lose our flight. So I waited for what seemed like an eternity, probably only about five minutes, until I felt a variety of explosions racing through my body.

Not knowing what to do or where I was in the airport, I raced outside, where I vomited... and had diarrhea simultaneously, painting the Mexican sidewalk a variety of colors, but everybody around me seemed to not be phased at all. I raced to the bathroom. And from that point your story is the same as my memory.

Perhaps it is my recognition that I will not become famous in any other way, or perhaps it's my hours of watching the Jerry Springer show, but either way reading this story does not embarrass me. I need to run, nature's calling.

Adam

There is much I can say here, about memory, and diarrhea of course, not to mention what could easily be perceived as a case study on how to be, and not be, an ugly American, but I think it's most important to note that this is something we shared, and it is now as ingrained piece of the ever-unfolding story about our family, as the time my mom bent time and space in the Everglades.

We didn't do over-the-counter medicines or bland foods, we didn't have rules, we were rarely careful as children, or necessarily even cared for all of the time, but we had love, lots of it, and adventure, and we now have stories, many, and a shared history we all revel in.

And who wouldn't kill for all of that, despite the trade-offs?

No one I know.

THE THING BEFORE THE THING

I am hunkered down at a long table at The Bottom Line in Greenwich Village. I am in my early twenties and I am waiting patiently for it to happen.

What is it?

I will tell you in a minute, because this part is about the thing before the thing.

The thing before the thing is that as I sit there milking my watery Gin & Tonic, tracing the sweaty trickles of condensation with my finger as it slides down the side of my glass, and as I try to be patient, or at least not a stalkerish freak, I feel someone place their hands on my shoulders and then lean over me to get a better look at the still empty stage.

I look up to see who it is, not that I expect I will know.

And yet as it turns out, I do know who it is. Not

personally, but I do know, and how couldn't I, with his clunky glass, beard, crazy Jew hair and bemused grin?

It's Allen Ginsberg, yes that Allen Ginsberg.

He smiles at me and then he walks away.

Why is this important?

For one, because I am a terrible starfucker and Allen fucking Ginsberg has just touched me, then smiled.

But that's not the most important thing.

No, what's important is that Allen Ginsberg is at The Bottom Line to read that night and I had no idea that was the case.

How couldn't I know that?

Because I am there to see Jim Carroll, he is the thing before the thing, and I had no idea, because no writer is more important to me than Jim Carroll.

I love him.

I love him like women my age love John Cusack. And why is that, because John Cusack speaks to them, and yes, Jim Carroll speaks to me in much the same way John Cusack speaks to them.

They don't know John Cusack, but through watching him in *Say Anything*, certainly, *The Sure Thing*, possibly, and *Serendipity,* maybe, fuck, Christ, John Cusack inhabits something, an ideal of some kind—funny, passionate, tall, and crazed about the women he loves—and everyone wants crazed, until they get it anyway.

Like them, I don't know Jim Carroll, technically I now know Allen Ginsberg better than Jim Carroll, but Jim Carroll wrote *The Basketball Diaries*, and nothing before *The Basketball Diaries* ever spoke to me like *The Basketball Diaries* did.

I re-read books as a boy, I was ravenous for words and the escape and balm they provided, and some books filled the chasm for me again, and again, *Carrie*, *The Catcher in the Rye*, *The Outsiders*, *Flowers in the Attic*, the *John Carter : Warlord of Mars* series, *The Chocolate War*, and so many others, but none of them was *The Basketball Diaries*.

It was electric, and real time, all live wire, and nerve endings, a mash-up of masturbation, drugs, sports, underage sex, predators, crime, writing, hustle, art, New York City in the mid-1960's, and people love to talk about cities, especially New York City as characters in stories, but usually they don't know what the fuck they're talking about. Here though New York City was oozing and fresh, and another breathing slice of a book, that was so graphic, vivid, and fraught with gunk and stickiness, it was like watching a documentary.

To this day I remember when Jim Carroll jerks-off on the roof of his building under the stars.

The college scout Bennie who wants to blow him.

The twins Winkie and Binkie who he wants to fuck, and how he worries that he chose the wrong twin after one sister strips for another guy, before realizing they must look the same.

The date that won't sleep with him, and keeps insisting there's a time and place for everything, until it actually is the time and place.

How Jim Carroll would cliff dive into the Harlem River while dodging the shit and scumbags floating by.

The girlfriend who gets him hard during gym class in Central Park—which leads him to picture an old woman's varicose veins because in hopes of killing his erection because he isn't wearing underwear.

The fact that he played basketball with Lew Alcindor, yes that Lew Alcindor.

The drugs he consumed, the uppers and downers, the endless marijuana and the heroin.

His haunting and prescient trenchcoated fantasies where he guns down his classmates out of pure boredom.

And then there is the language, fluid, poetic and crass, a twisty mix of slang and detail, all piling-up on itself, until it becomes something more than language, something visual, a fever dream, or overture, filled with spiky notes, and jazz beats.

I imagine it would have been impossible not to be taken with all of this when I was twelve and first got the book from my friend Adam, but looking back I must have wondered if this was what the future could hold, girls and sports and grit and hustle and living in New York City, and the idea that like Icarus, Jim Carroll may have flown too close to the sun, wings melting, and fraught with plummet, yet somehow landed on his feet.

Jim Carroll was real, he was punk and he was legend.

I also think that over the years I must have somehow overlooked the second half of the book, where it's all junk and desperation, nodding out and Rykers Island.

I imagine that it didn't fit my narrative for Jim Carroll, or at least the Jim Carroll life I might have almost aspired to if I had any idea how anyone aspires to such a life.

And I know this because I recently re-read the book for the first time in twenty-five years.

I wanted to know if it still spoke to me.

I should say here, that when I saw Jim Carroll at The Bottom Line I was there with Adam who had been the one to first introduce me to *The Basketball Diaries* all those years ago.

I was at work, in New York City thank you very much, when the phone rang.

"Yo, meet me at The Bottom Line at 7:00, Jim Carroll is performing," Adam said.

Not reading mind you, *performing*.

As I have mentioned, we didn't even know Allen Ginsberg was going to be there, Allen fucking Ginsberg, but that was because we loved Jim Carroll, and everything else was ephemera, beautiful, and raging, but ephemera none-the-less.

On stage he was as Jim Carroll as you could ever want him to be, loose-limbed, and gaunt, all vibrato, and stalking the stage like a punk junkie spider, as he read some piece about his father, maybe, and a scorpion, definitely, and if it is true that this piece couldn't possibly touch the sacred text that is *The Basketball Diaries*, it didn't matter, he didn't really have to do anything but show-up.

Which for the most part is what he did for years, though not for much longer, because somewhere along the way, he stopped showing-up, and at the end, it was him living as a shut-in, and a memory, primarily kept alive, by his primary, not only, but primary legacy, *The Basketball Diaries*.

So, given that, how does it hang now?

Brilliant, and beautiful, as lyrical and raucous as ever, mostly, totally, I don't know. I still love it, and all those memories I had, they were all there, which made me happy.

It's funny though, reading it again now I'm amazed at how young he was, and so close to my age when I first read it, when he seemed so old, or worldly, or something.

The druggy stretches near the end get somewhat draggy and repetitive, even if they remain at times both sad and funny.

But there are still the girls and the basketball, and the

hustling, though I had forgotten just how far he was willing to go to make a buck. I remembered the stick-ups and the purse snatching, but I'm not sure I recalled his working as a john.

The pages are still alive and humming though like few things I've read since, *Fear and Loathing in Las Vegas*, *Cruddy*, *We The Animals*, and *Bastard Out of Carolina*, come close, very, but they're not like this, not like a movie wrapping itself around my brain, first as a hug, and then as a bruise.

The book is also something else though, because there is one piece of *The Basketball Diaries* I somehow forgot about entirely—it's when he writes about becoming a writer.

It's impossible to read it now, and not think, there, right there, thirty-five years ago, something was set in motion for me, something started there, and I'm not even remotely sure that I knew it was.

Later, and when I was now living in Chicago, Jim Carroll came to perform at Lounge Axe. He was older than when I saw him at The Bottom Line, still lanky and gaunt, and still Jim Carroll, but barely anyone was there, and I didn't see Allen Ginsberg anywhere.

He read the same piece he read when I saw him read in New York City and I felt sad.

He seemed stuck in place, and after many years of being stuck myself, I was finally not, not really, I was writing, and it wasn't clear that he still was.

Then one day he was dead, a sickly, skeletal, shut–in who never quite finished his final book.

Maybe it couldn't end any other way for him, not when he had flown so high and so bright, and maybe it doesn't matter, he was a poet, and he was a punk god, he survived the junk, and the hustle, and the streets of New York City, he changed lives, he wrote *The Basketball Diaries*, and what more do we need from him?

I don't know, but I do know that he had once made us feel like more was possible, that the hustle was beautiful, and that a poet can emerge from the streets, and isn't that enough for any one life time?

THE 1990's

RUNNING FROM A DREAM

This is a tale that unfolds in three acts.

In the first act I am out running. It is a crisp and foggy day, an upstate New York kind of day. The dew is glistening on every leaf, the grass is slick, and it is so hazy, that except for the runners, everything seems to be moving in slow motion. I can see myself running in this place, and it takes me back to high school cross-country days past, and towns like Montrose and Baldwinsville.

Back in those days I glided through wooded paths, never losing my breath or feeling the strain of the effort in my knees and back.

In fact, as I observe myself out there all fluid motion

and composure, I should probably sense that something is awry—the person I'm watching is not me, or at least not me anymore.

That is not the twenty-nine year old body I lug around these days fruitlessly trying to recapture some of my former glory.

No, that is me at sixteen or eighteen or whenever that is not now.

I guess I should realize this, but I don't, I am too caught up in the moment and the feeling of how free I once felt.

As I think about this image it's ironic, really.

The person I am watching seems so full of power and grace, yet I now know that to be a deception of sorts. As powerful as I look and as calm as I appear to be, it's all a bit of a facade. That person ran as fast and far as he could, hoping it would allow him to escape the anxieties that ruled his days and nights.

Running was his outlet.

Unfortunately, outside of reading, and a brief moment when I, he, wrote, it was his only outlet, and it was a temporary one at that, but he, I mean I, didn't realize that at the time, I just kept running.

Of course, in the moment, and as I find myself caught up in this out of body experience I am not thinking about running as escape. No, I am truly awestruck at how I once looked, and I lose myself in the images of another time and place.

Hence, the shock of Act Two.

Act Two finds me as I am now: older and somewhat bewildered.

I am no longer running, instead I am in a doctor's office, and this doctor is telling me that I have a heart condition, that electronically, something is off, and that he really has no explanation for why this is.

I hear him saying this, and yet it makes no sense to me.

I was just running, I keep saying to myself, and not just running, but gliding really.

Meanwhile, even as I am thinking this, he is telling me that it is not safe for me to run anymore, and if I must, I shouldn't run far, may be two to three miles, and definitely not alone, never alone.

The problem here is that he may be saying all this, but I'm not quite getting it.

Wasn't I just out running?

I start to panic a little.

Maybe that wasn't really me out there running, but what the hell is this? How did I get into this office and why is it all so confusing?

I feel as if I have fallen into a pit, and though I am desperately reaching for branches and handholds, I just keep missing them.

The confusion is further exacerbated by the frustration of trying to get any good answers, or really any answers at all, from the doctor.

I keep asking him questions, as does Debbie, sometimes simultaneously, but he continues to say nothing that means anything to us.

We become horribly desperate, practically begging him for anything that will enlighten us, but he seems to have nothing to give.

Our desperation is particularly palpable next to his calmness.

Or is it coldness?

Meanwhile, underlying the feeling of panic and bewilderment is this sense that somehow I am to blame for this, that I have done something to bring this on me, that I could have been more careful along the way.

"Was it the drugs?" I ask.

The doctor won't say yes and he won't say no. He won't quite commit to anything.

It becomes obvious that we are not going to learn any details about my condition. I am sick now and that's it. A judgment has been passed and life will no longer be the same for me, regardless of what questions I ask or choices I make.

Ultimately it is so fucking frustrating, so fucking unbelievable and difficult to comprehend, that I am reduced to tears, and as the tears flow, I suddenly find myself in a large, empty warehouse fraught with dust and shadows.

I am lying there, naked and exposed, and my mother is holding me, seemingly having materialized at the moment I need her most.

The fact is, there will be no running today, if ever again.

And then I hear the alarm, and we are on to Act Three.

I quickly realize that this is a bad dream, but it's hard to tell exactly what's going on.

It's so very dark, and so very early, and as I fall back to sleep, repeatedly hitting doze on my alarm clock, I feel like I keep falling right back into the dream's desperation and confusion.

When I finally do wake, I am obsessed with capturing every detail of the experience.

I begin to write it down during breakfast, and then I continue to write about it in the icy bowels of the train station.

I don't even stop after getting on the train itself.

I finish as the sun is coming up and the elevated train I am riding emerges from Chicago's dank underground tunnels.

I find myself looking at what I have written through-out the day, and trying to make sense of the images and messages at hand.

What does it all mean?

Is it that I am feeling older and more easily scared these days?

Am I sensing that it is time to truly revisit my lost youth and its corresponding anxieties?

Have I suppressed my true feelings about my father's undiagnosed heart condition?

Or is it some combination thereof, a morass of confusion, fear and the ever-present sense that we are only so free, and will inevitably found ourselves plummeting to Earth?

Try as I might, I cannot make sense of any of it. I don't seem to have the tools or capabilities to process what I have experienced.

I never did learn them.

As I ponder all this I know there is only one means for dealing with the state this dream has left me in, the one thing that rarely fails me in times of need, confusion or escape.

So, when I get home I lace up my running shoes and I head out into the night.

At first I feel slow and winded. My legs are tight and I can't find my rhythm. Quickly though, as always, my steps become light, and at least for the moment the day's concerns begin to melt away.

Soon I am all-knowing, all-powerful, and at peace.

And with that, Act Three ends like Act One began—I am fluid grace and motion, I have left confusion and chaos in the dust and I have temporarily found respite from my anxieties.

THE NATURAL

I never got baseball, and I never understood why it was fun.

Why did someone choose to stand around and wait for a ball that might never come? Soccer made sense.

It was full of action and contact and human drama, but baseball, sorry no, did not get it.

The problem though is that when you're a twelve-year old boy you have to play baseball. You had to play in upstate New York in the 1980's, anyway.

So, I would try out year after disheartening year for little league, hating every minute of it and vowing never to come out again.

The first year I tried out, me and all the other sweaty-faced little kids were sent to the outfield for fielding drills. It was a terribly humid night as we waited for the big, booming surely-impossible-to-catch fly balls to come our way.

We prayed for cloud cover and waved our oversized gloves at the marauding army of gnats that gladly flew around our heads, dive-bombed our ears and buried themselves in the corner of our eyes.

The field was next to the elementary school I attended. Rumor had it that the school had been built on top of a swamp to save money and because of this it sank something like one quarter inch per year into the ground.

I checked on this constantly, but never once noticed a discernable difference.

Anyway, we were all lined-up and as I waited for my turn I grew increasingly nervous.

How should I hold my glove exactly?

Should I use two hands?

Is it best to charge the ball or let it come to you?

I didn't know, not any of it, and there I was with all these questions and no answers, and suddenly it was my turn, the ball was in the air, and while I didn't think for a moment that I would be able to catch it, I started sizing it up just in case.

At first it was real tiny, just another star in the upstate New York night, but then as I drew a bead on it, it began to get bigger and bigger, and soon I was not so scared, it actually looked catchable.

I might have caught it, too.

But just as I was about to reel it in, a girl ran out from behind me on line, made the perfect catch and drew a huge round of applause from all those watching.

A girl.

After that I couldn't catch a thing and all I really wanted to do was go home, which eventually I did only to break down in tears as soon as I saw my dad.

The next year we were participating in batting drills on the soccer field on the other side of the school. The soccer field faced the neighborhood church where all of the after school fights were held. On the side of the church was this enormous neon sign that was on 24 hours a day and read "Jesus Saves." I was sure the sign had something to do with banking, but I never got up the nerve to ask anyone how it all worked.

Regardless, there we were, and there I was, basically awaiting my chance to slink out quietly into the night.

I felt I could hit if given the chance, but I also knew that I couldn't hit very far, and I had never had to hit under any kind of pressure.

Then something funny happened.

The fat dad-looking guy who was pitching to us threw me this really slow pitch, I made contact—the crack of the ball like a tree-branch snapping—and the ball nearly took off fat dad's head in the process.

The tryouts came to a stop as he got up from the ground, and with everyone watching, I sauntered off to the next set of drills.

Well, I believe it was a saunter, I might have ambled. Whatever I thought was cool at the time, certainly.

Just like the almost catch the year before that one hit might have been the start of something.

I was drafted by one of the teams in the league and there's no doubt it was due to that hit. The problem is that being drafted is only a good thing if you actually know you have been.

But I never quite found out that I had been drafted, at least not in a timely fashion.

As it turned out, the coach tried calling my house for a week, but we didn't have an answering machine at the time, and no one was ever really home back then, and so I never received the call telling me I had been drafted and that practice was starting.

In fact, I might have never found out at all, but for the father of some other kid in the neighborhood who told me that the team was down to its final practice and I should probably try to make an appearance if I hoped to play at all.

I went to that last practice, but the coach wasn't so cool when I got there.

"How is it," he said, "that I can never get hold of

anyone at your house?"

I couldn't answer that.

"And how do you expect to make the team when you haven't been to any practices," he continued.

I couldn't answer that question either.

Nor could I really prove myself that night—I was too anxious to field balls, too flustered to pitch and way too self-conscious to bat.

"You can play in the B league if you want to," the coach said after practice, "not that there's a full schedule or anything."

I didn't respond, A league, B league, whatever, this sucked.

"Oh, and there aren't any hats left either," he added. "You will need to get one for yourself."

Which was fine, anything was, I just wanted to leave.

I didn't care, I hated the whole thing, and I was re- lieved to play in the B league where no one would see me strike out, or worse, watch some girl run out in front of me to catch a fly ball.

And that might have been the end of it—I played some B league games, I got some hits—and I would have been okay with that.

But there is a reason they make bad after school spe- cials—much of life really is like a bad after school spe- cial—and so in the tradition of bad after school specials throughout time—think of just about anything starring Lance Kerwin, Helen Hunt, Scott Baio, you get the picture—the coach invited the B team players to come sit on the bench for the last game of the season.

He wasn't promising anything of course, say actual playing time for example, but if we wanted to check it out, it was fine with him.

So I went. I sat there at the end of the bench and I watched the team fall behind like 10-0 as everyone else slowly got in but me.

And once again I was pretty much okay with all of it.

This was my destiny—a mélange of disappointment, swallowing my pride and telling myself everything was alright.

But then the last inning came around and the coach inexplicably decided that I should have a chance to bat.

Now, if this had truly been an after school special, or at least one of the *Bad News Bears* sequels, I would have walked up to bat and spanked the ball far into the night sky.

Fireworks would have probably gone off.

My teammates would have mobbed me at home plate.

The coach would have said something like, "Damn, I had your soccer playing fairy ass figured all wrong kid, you're alright."

Then we would have gone out for pizza and maybe, just maybe, I would have kissed the girl too, someone like

Jodie Foster, or at least someone like Kristy McNichol, playing the Jodie Foster type.

All of which would have been very good indeed, but this was real life, or at least something approximating it, so instead, my legs were rubbery as I walked to the plate, the bat seemed unbelievably heavy, and I was sweating so much that the combination of the cool night air and my now boundless anxiety was causing my teeth to chatter uncontrollably.

Soon I was standing in the batter's box and the field looked just enormous and imposing.

On top of all that, the pitcher was a bully I knew from school.

Of course.

He was tall and menacing, sloppy, with terrible Pep-peroni pizza skin that I could see glistening under the lights, even as he appeared to be standing a million miles away.

Still, I tried to focus on him when he went into his pitching motion, I really did, and I tried to concentrate on the ball when he released it, but it was so small, and it was moving so fast, and it just flew by me before I even had a chance to lift the bat off my shoulder.

Ball One.

Which was good, but then before I could collect my-self the second pitch came whistling by me. Ball Two. Also good, though at this point I looked out at the pitcher, and I vowed to myself that I would swing at the next pitch no matter what.

He, in turn, looked right back at me and as I found myself caught up in his stare he let the third pitch go, I was so stunned that once again the bat never even left my shoulder.

Ball Three.

It was around this time that I started to think that I was probably going to get on base whether I bothered to swing the bat or not—what were the chances that he was going to strike me out before throwing another ball?

Pretty slim, I thought, and that was a good outcome, right?

I might not get a hit, but the idea was to get on base, wasn't it?

Maybe if I just played it cool from that point on I could draw a walk, take my base, and be thought of as a patient batter, a guy who wasn't going to swing at a bad pitch and hurt the team because I was caught up in my own needs and statistics.

I didn't plan to get so lost in my thoughts.

But I did.

Nor did I expect him to release that fourth pitch quite so quickly.

But he did.

And once again I didn't even muster a swing.

Which could have been embarrassing, and could have really sucked, but luckily I was too stunned to be embarrassed, plus, it was Ball Four and I was told to take my base.

When I got there, I immediately noticed that something had changed—the game had somehow taken on a whole new look.

The grass was so much greener, and the dirt was dirtier, everything was vibrant, alive.

But it was more than that.

The field didn't look quite so big anymore, nor did things seem to be moving quite so fast out there, either.

I could now follow the pitcher's movements as he slowly went into his motion and the ball didn't even really seem to get to home plate all that quickly from out there.

I could also see that the infielders were moving in a kind of slow motion as well—lulled by the time it took the pitch to reach the batter, and the fact that they didn't really know whether there would be a hit, much less where it was going.

Furthermore, it struck me as I stood there that there was probably no way they could prevent me from stealing second base.

Was the catcher really going to catch that pitch and then rifle it to the second baseman in time to throw me out?

No, not a chance, and so I took off, head down, arms pumping, heels slapping me in the butt, dust everywhere, before sliding feet first, the throw so late I was practically standing again when it reached us.

Now I was on second base and there was this hum in the air, like electricity, and I was so very lost in it, lost in my own world, following my own rhythm and bending the game to my will, and not the opposite, not any more, anyway.

I felt like a God.

This is where I belonged. Out at night under the lights. Stealing bases. Running with reckless abandon.

It was fast, physical, totally liberating and it was my destiny.

I stole third base as well, easily, and awesomely, and there I was staring at home plate, and in control, and loving baseball, when boom, the guy at bat laced one into the gap between the center fielder and the left fielder, and I was gone, taking off for home, scoring with ease and bringing in our first run.

Which, let's be honest, was very cool indeed.

Yes, it was true that I had been too scared to swing the bat, but I had stolen two bases and I had scored a run and what do you think about that?

I thought that ruled, and I was flying, and that high might have stayed just that, a high, something to ride for a little while, to reflect on, and talk about over pizza with the Jodie Foster look-a-like as I looked towards the next season and all of the possibilities that awaited me.

But it wasn't to be.

The coach wasn't smiling.

"Where do you get off stealing bases?" he shouted. "I never once flashed the steal sign?"

He looked like he was in pain.

What is a steal sign I wanted to ask, but I was too scared to do so.

And hadn't I scored?

Apparently that didn't matter.

There was a sign, and you didn't steal unless you saw that sign, which evidently I should have known.

But I didn't know.

I hadn't played with the team all season, attended a practice or game or ever been told what the sign was, much less that such a thing as steal signs even existed.

But I didn't mention any of this.

Instead I tried to savor this small victory of mine, ignore the coach and think ahead to the magical next season that was already looming so large in my head.

All night and into the next day in fact, all I thought about was baseball, steal signs, hits and scoring runs. It all seemed so real, and so possible, and right there in front of me. This was my *actual* destiny, if I could just figure out how to grab it.

All of which would have been really nice, and just the kind of redemption arc that after school specials have so ably illustrated since the beginning of time, or at least the 1970's.

Enter the bully pitcher.

We were in the cafeteria, and he was coming right at me, impossible to avoid.

He was huge and greasy in his ill-fitting T-shirt as he planted himself right in front of me, his pimply prepubescent face contorted into a malevolent grin.

"You should know," he said, "that my coach told me to walk you because he felt sorry for you, and so I did, which means you didn't earn it, and I wanted to be sure you knew that."

I would like to tell you that I told him, "who the fuck cares what you did, I stole two bases and I can play baseball, and next year at this time when you're off in jail, or in some juvie home somewhere I will be back and I will be king of the motherfucking world, so fuck you you pizza faced motherfucker."

But I didn't say that or anything else.

Nor did I play little league the next year, because after I went to the tryouts, again, the same coach drafted me, again, and he told me that I had to choose between little league and soccer, because I was at an age where I really needed to start concentrating on one sport.

I had already lost what little interest I had in little league that previous fall in the lunchroom though, and once again I was trying out for little league because I felt like I had to.

But now I didn't have to, now I had to make a choice.

"Fine," I said, "soccer it is."

After that, I moved on with my life.

And I did move on, really, mostly, and I would like to tell you that those series of experiences had no ill affect on me, that I never thought about little league much after that because despite the bully and the fact that I never got a hit, I really had moved on, stronger and more confident.

But that's just not exactly true, which I know that you and everyone who has ever watched an after school special of any kind knows as well.

It's not that the "we feel sorry for you" walk haunted me day in and day out as much as that at bat come to find itself grouped-in with all the other feelings of powerlessness I carried—and still carry—with me from childhood into adulthood.

It was just one more thing that had totally sucked and that I never failed to think about when I was, and yes, sometimes, am, feeling especially bad about myself.

It was also something I was never be able to rectify, and few things are worse than that, the things one can't fix, because you are no longer a kid, and so how would that work?

How indeed?

Because there I am one crispy San Francisco night, it is the early 1990's and I'm stepping into the batter's box for the first time since that very last time so many years before.

I can't even say exactly what I am doing there.

The law firm I work at has a softball team that needs a few extra guys to fill out the roster. The season has just started, and they don't really need me to do more than sit on the bench. It is a lot like little league really, still, they are basically a good bunch of guys and I am far from home, and I'm not twelve anymore, so why not.

On this particular night the team is losing and they are looking for something, some kind of spark, anything to get them going, and they ask me to bat.

I head out to home plate, I raise the bat to my shoulder, and I look out across the great expanse of field staring back at me.

On the one hand it is not much different than that night in little league so long ago.

It is dark and there is a slight chill in the air.

There is a pitcher out there, and there is me trying to figure out why I am even in this position in the first place.

On the other hand, it is like night and day.

There is nothing remotely scary about it.

The pitcher is just some old guy from some other firm with a bunch of kids, a mini-van and a mortgage.

Things are moving much slower as well.

So slow really that as I stand there I am acutely aware of the seams on the ball as the pitcher seeks the correct grip and the little tufts of dust that rise each time the second baseman moves in anticipation for what might or might not happen next.

Then the pitch is in the air and I am watching it rotate towards me, all big and slow, and I find myself just waiting on it.

I get the bat off my shoulder in plenty of time, and I swing away, level and confident and knowing.

There is contact, the crack of bat meeting ball, and the ball just sails away from me and over the outstretched hands of the second baseman.

At first I am just watching the arc of the ball as it looks for some space to roll into the outfield, which is enormous and never-ending.

But then I am running, and I know that I am easily safe at first base, but I also think about how the team will benefit from a double, and so I go for it, and now I am flying, and then there is a throw as I slide hard into second base, and it's all chaos and dust for a moment.

Then I am up and I am brushing the dirt off my bloodied shin and I am safe at second.

The team starts to cheer.

The crowd starts to cheer.

And I just stand there grinning absurdly and taking it all in.

It really is something.

And for a moment I find myself in some other time and some other place, and it's like I am standing out on top of that swamp, Jesus Saves illuminating the night sky.

It's pretty cool right then, and fuck it if for that moment, I'm not king of the world after all.

BACK HOME

There was this boy with his head in your lap.

Which is not exactly what it sounds like, though depending on how that sounds to you, it isn't exactly not that either.

Which is to say that he isn't a little boy, you have those now and you know what they look like, he was more like a young man, as were you, it's just that you just weren't as young as he was, with his boyish face, pale skin, and light, near translucent scruff.

But you're getting ahead of yourself, that is the present, or that present anyway, and this doesn't work without knowing the past and the decisions you made that got you from there to here.

Because before that, there was a door, though not exactly a door, it was more like a passage, both in the metaphorical sense certainly, as in it takes you somewhere both new and old all at once—a sort of a *Raiders of the Lost Ark* "take a step and the bridge will appear" kind of passage—but also in a literal sense, because there is also a curtain, and behind it a long hall in a club South of Market in San Francisco that no one in the club seems to be paying attention to, except for you and your friends.

Now how can that be?

You don't know, but San Francisco has always been like that for you.

Or, it was like that anyway, because you don't live there anymore, you live in New York City now, you live back home, and San Francisco is now a place you used to live, a place you once ran to, but then ran away from.

There had been this morning, gray, drizzly, and all upstate New York. And when was that? It was before the boy, and before you ran west only to return again. It could have been decades earlier, but it was only 1990, and so only two or three years prior to now.

So, there you were, climbing out of bed at dawn, the drugs and alcohol still lingering and pooling on your brain like the morning dew on the grass below the window you are staring out of.

The rain and the old houses with their peeling paint and faded siding stretch on forever, a view you had taken in every morning of every day of your life up until now, and there was the feeling of both being nowhere and falling down a pit, desperately grabbing at the stray branches all around you, yet unable to grab one regardless of how hard you tried.

"California," you said to no one in particular, because it seemed like that's where people go when they need to go wherever people go to become something new.

Then you were living there.

And now you are not.

Except that now you are back again, though only for a long weekend and now you are thinking about whether you made the right choice when you left.

You never stopped thinking about that then.

What if you hadn't left?

What if your mother hadn't been diagnosed with breast cancer?

What if your grandfather hadn't felt forced to move into a retirement community before he was ready to do so? What if you didn't think about your girlfriend all the time, or hadn't been doing so since the day you met her, even when you, or she, really didn't want you to?

What if?

And what sort of precipice had you been on while you were still living here? Because that's part of it too, you never felt like you were on the precipice of anything here, nothing made sense.

You just knew that you loved living in San Francisco, the burritos, the drugs, the ultimate Frisbee, Muir Woods, Highway One, Santa Cruz, the Grateful Dead, the Raves, the drugs, Stinson Beach, the fog enveloping the bay when you woke-up in the morning.

But these things are not quite an actual life. Not for you anyway.

Because where was it all going?

You didn't know, and you couldn't figure it out, just like you can't figure out now why you can't ever find the distance you need from yourself to make sense of things where you actually are, or were, and instead believe you need to run away to do so.

Of course, maybe that's what you're saying here, now, and not on the trip back then, but in your present day head, revising and tweaking the past, and trying to create a narrative that fits your current day perception of who you were and are, or want to be, and been?

Maybe, you are no more reliable than any other narrator you write about? Maybe that's not how it all went down, and yet, that's how you remember it, and that's how it feels now, and that must mean something, right?

"We're going to SOMA, and we have X," your friend says.

You have only landed hours in San Francisco before, it's late, you are tired and high and drunk and manic, but who are you to argue with an offer like that?

That's not even a real question.

You're not going to argue with that, you never did back then.

And why would you on that trip anyway, it's why you're back there, to recapture something, and remember what it is you think you miss, right?

Right.

Now even before all of that, before you left, and before you go back, there is a guy at the office you work with in Oakland.

He's the new guy.

You were once the new guy.

The young one.

The cute one.

The one older female supervisors scheduled closed door meetings with and said, "Do you think people will talk," as they told you how emasculated their husbands were.

The one co-worker's smiled at in the copy room, lingering briefly to stare, before they said, "If I wasn't queer..." The one who a colleague cornered in the file room before saying, "I could rape you right here, right now," no smile, not at first, and no joke.

You were that guy, until you weren't, because then the new guy came, younger, cuter and new.

Was he smarter than you? No, not necessarily.

Was he more professional? Maybe.

Was he better at his job? Not so much.

But he's new, and you are not, not any more.

You realize how much you like being the guy, and now that you're not, what's left, softball with the older guys in the office, and the job itself, a job which is crap, and something that is not what you want or ever aspire to do, work for the sake of work.

And so where does that leave you?

Nowhere, with no idea how to fix it, which when you think about it, is no different than that rainy day in upstate New York two years before.

You get to the bar in SOMA. It's young, loud, and frat boy. You think, here, this, why?

"Don't worry," your friend says, sensing your confusion, "just follow me."

You walk across the dance floor, dodging young men and women, and as you do, it gets darker and darker. Soon you're facing a curtain in the back corner of the bar, and after a moment, your friend pulls the curtain aside to reveal a long hall which she quickly darts into.

You follow her, the X starting to kick-in, and when did you take that anyway, you don't know, and it doesn't matter, what matters, is that you're chasing your friend and in doing so you bump into the woman in front of you. Not that you're sure where she appeared from, but she did, and she's wearing this impossibly short white dress, and her legs are so long, which you love so much, and her skin is glowing, and skin you love even more than long legs, though especially on X.

You stumble and you grab the woman by the hips as you try to steady yourself, and she turns, startled, and looks at you.

"I'm so sorry," you mumble, trying not to stare at her legs or touch her.

She is like Dazzler, her skin suddenly radiating over you in shock waves.

"It's okay sugar," she says smiling.

Though she is not a she, she is a he and he is beautiful.

And then she is gone, just like that, spectral, and vanished, and your friend is now at a door, beckoning you to follow her, and the music is suddenly pulsating from all sides, the walls reverberating, something you can see, and feel, little sine waves rippling all around you, and you are carried off on them, leaping from beat to beat and trying to catch-up.

There is this afternoon before you move back to New York when you are lying in the backseat of a friend's car as you drive south down Highway 1 from San Francisco to Santa

Cruz. The car is gliding along above the craggy cliffs that drop onto the endless onslaught of waves below, their spray taking flight into space before settling into the blue waters, back home, albeit only briefly before starting their journey again, and on into perpetuity, a watery Sysiphus.

The sun is high and brilliant and it bisects the back seat of the car, half your face baked in the rays being refracted through the window, the other half nestled in the shadows. And you are high, always high then, taking bat hits and lolling about as the Grateful Dead courses through the speakers above and around you.

You are wracked with anxiety though and trying to run from it at every turn. You are leaving for New York in just weeks and you cannot quite believe it is a good idea.

"California, preaching on the burning shore
California, I'll be knocking on the golden door
Like an angel, standing in a shaft of light
Rising up to paradise, I know I'm gonna shine."

Estimated Prophet joins the waves and the sun and Highway 1, all of this Northern California goodness wrapping itself around your brain, and you think about the last Grateful Dead show you will be hitting before you go. It's a Mardi Gras show just days from now, and you decide that if they play *Estimated Prophet*, you will not move home, the

Grateful Dead will be sending you a message and you will embrace it.

You go to the show, you paint your face in the parking lot, you pull your hair back into a ponytail and you consume copious amounts of mushrooms as you wander among the T-shirt vendors and burrito sellers that comprise the tent city which has taken root in the parking lot. The Grateful Dead do not play *Estimated Prophet* that night, and whether you would have really stayed or not even if they had, you don't, you move back home as planned.

You push through the door at the end of the hall and you enter a warehouse of some kind, where there is throbbing, seizure inducing lights that envelope the entire room in a sonic hug; massive murals of superheroes cover the walls, The Incredible Hulk and Captain America, looming and colorful, threatening and protective all at once; music, techno and thumping, which is so loud and so percussive, the notes land like body blows, relentless, loving and ultimately overwhelming; and an array of beautiful, androgynous boys and girls, smooth skinned, short-haired, and high cheek-boned, dancing like it's the end of the world, the lights creating a slow motion haze of bodies and skin.

There is also stadium style seating reminiscent of a small town high school gym above the dance floor, and you opt for that, making your way to the top to sit down, the X, the skin, the lights, and the long flight and day, conspiring to push you into a voyeuristic and gelatinous blob, soaking up everything around you, even as you, congeal into an unmoving and saturated mass.

You sit there staring into the scrum of bodies below you, and the boys and girls start to undress, pressing into one another, and merging into a naked, pulsating, slow motion sex hive, a perpetual buzz of motion.

Soon it's all boys, the girls now gone, or maybe they were never there at all, because can you even trust yourself to know what you've been watching, then, much less now, no, you can't, not really.

As you sit staring at the random body parts floating into the air, the boy walks-up, he's wearing a dark hoodie and T-shirt, his hair is short, his skin awash in the lights and he is glowing. He sits down next to you, mumbles something about MDMA and Special K, and then puts his head in your lap.

You stroke his hair, and as you float above the orgy, the music pounding, you think about how this is the life here, the only version you know anyway; how it is not the one you have chosen to live, however, instead choosing to focus on family, stability, responsibility and career; and how in this moment it's all so very tortuous.

One night while you are still living in San Francisco you

are doing countless bong hits in your living room with a bunch of friends, and the moment slowly morphs into a euphoric need for pints of Ben & Jerry's Cherry Garcia and Chunky Monkey ice cream, which also become countless in their destruction, and after hours of smoking and ice cream and laughter and *Sports Center*, you find yourself staring out the window, searching for something, and off in the distance, hovering and majestic you make out the contours of the Golden Gate Bridge.

"We should run to the Golden Gate Bridge," you say, and no one questions that.

And so you run, no one talking, step after step, the weed and ice cream fading into a sweet memory of another time and place, so long before now. The streets are empty, the night still, perfect, but you never get there, the bridge always lingering just beyond your collective reach, beckoning, but nowhere, and eventually you turn around, breakfast and work looming, and you are happy, and sated, but no more clear about anything than you were hours before.

The day after the warehouse and the dancing and the X, as you meander, exhausted and joyful, you see the boy from the night before, wasted and skinny, and wandering the streets, and you think again about paths and precipices and doors, and how life in San Francisco for you, was, and is, full of joy and wonder, but in the light of day, also seems false and lacking.

You are also reminded that nothing makes sense to you here, and that while this may turn out to be the case anywhere and everywhere you ever go, back home at least you may actually be on the edge of something, and that whatever it is, and however torturous and confusing it is to figure it out, for now it's there, not here, hovering somewhere and waiting for you.

THE SUBWAY STORIES

I did not grow-up in New York City, and so I did not take the subway to school, parties, or sporting events. And because of this I do not have the subway map memorized and don't know which series of trains will get me to Far Rockaway when I find myself standing on East 98th and Madison.

Nor do I intuitively know where to position myself on the platform at the West 96th Street stop so I can exit the 2 train near the stairwell at Times Square.

But that's okay, because I will learn it all, I have moved to New York City, I now ride the trains endlessly and I love every minute of it.

From the ancient gum embedded on the platforms in every station to the ceilings that drip murky water in every hall and tunnel that connect them, and from the vendors selling socks on every train line to the homeless asking for change after breaking into song, the New York City subways have more stories per moment than any other place I've ever been.

And these are my stories.

I am heading to the office on Friday morning my first week on the job as a caseworker. I am carrying a large overnight bag with me because I plan to head out of town that night after work.

I catch the 3 train at 96th Street and I head south to the Times Square/42nd Street stop where I need to catch the 7 train to my office.

The station is packed when I get there, full of guys in black leather coats and sweatpants; women in fuchsia business suits and Reebok workout shoes; and young men, black, white, Hispanic, and Asian in baggy Phat Farm jeans and Timberlands.

Everyone is pushing one another, and pushing me, as they race to their respective trains, and my bag is constantly slipping off of my shoulder as I try to right myself in the tidal wave of bodies around me.

I head to the stairwell that will take me down to the platform where the 7 train is already approaching and as I do I work my way past a newsstand that is covered with lurid NY Post cover stories about heads being found in hotel rooms; issues old and new of *Elle* and *Vogue* with their too skinny, waif-like Kate Moss clones and endless copies of *Playboy*, *Screw*, *Big Busts* and *Stud*.

The stairwell is convulsing with people and I am at a virtual standstill when a burly, mustachioed guy behind me starts to yell.

"Hey, c'mon already, the fucking train is right there," he says.

"What do you want me to do," I say, "look at all these people in front of me?"

"What do I want you do," he says, "you got that big bag, knock someone the fuck over."

I do not respond and we do not catch our train.

Its five o'clock and it's very warm out.

I get on the 1 train heading towards the Bronx and am immediately assaulted by the air conditioning, the contrast in temperatures sure to lead to a summer cold.

The train is packed and I have my bag hanging over my shoulder.

I'm holding the pole with my left hand, and reading *Newsday* with my right.

A young couple starts to argue off to my left by the door.

"Yo, fuck you man!" the brown-haired girl in the tight jeans says actively gesticulating with her right index finger to make her point. "You suck."

"Fuck me? Fuck you!" the dark-haired guy in the black hooded sweatshirt replies, barely moving an eyelash much less a muscle.

I think to myself about how this is the classic subway pick-pocket situation.

Dumb-ass guy is reading his newspaper.

He is not paying attention to his surroundings, and not paying attention to his wallet because his hands are not free.

He gets distracted when two people start having an argument.

And when this occurs, a third person takes his wallet after he pretends to inadvertently bump into him.

I have read about this scenario over and over again, and it's brilliant in both its concept and execution. Successful pickpockets work like magicians, their mastery lying in their ability to create a diversion that shifts your attention just enough from the task at hand to make their move. But just because I know this about pickpockets, does not mean I think I'm above being victimized. Far from it, in fact not only am I certain that I could have my wallet stolen at any time, but I also recognize that this sort of knowledge means nothing, because I am not the type of person who is willing to take steps to protect myself.

I am not keeping my right hand in my pocket for

example where my wallet is, instead choosing to keep both of my hands tied-up with other things.

Nor am I avoiding the crowd by the door, much less fully paying attention to my surroundings, I am unwilling to move and I am reading the newspaper.

If anything, I am treating the whole situation as some kind of intellectual exercise.

And what happens?

What do you think?

As we arrive at the next station, I play it all out in my head and become distracted by the idea of being distracted, even though I know that being distracted is the last thing I should be.

The doors open, the couple continues to fight and another guy in a hooded sweatshirt bumps into me on his way out of the train.

I reach for my wallet, but it's gone, as are the couple and the guy who bumped into me, all of who have now blended into the exiting crowd.

Another day, another crowded train, this time the E train.

Everyone has packed in around the doors and I do my best to move into the aisle and towards the center of the train.

There is a big Ving Rhames-type dude standing in front of me though, unmoving and seemingly unmovable.

I cannot get around him unless he gives a little, but it's not clear whether that's ever going to happen.

I think about what I might say to him.

"Yo, Ving do you mind moving up some, or maybe letting me by, you know maybe giving a brother a little space?"

It sounds sincere and neighborly, but I'm not so sure it sounds convincing.

Ving may very well be willing to move, but he hasn't done so on his own despite the fact that the car is filling up around him.

He might respond of course to a conductor asking him to move along, or even a taped message regarding train courtesy, but none is forthcoming, and no one can follow what those taped messages say any way.

I wonder how best to proceed and decide to forget about the whole thing.

I soon find myself lost in one of those packed subway car kind of reveries, only to be abruptly snapped back to reality, by a smallish, fire hydrant of an older woman who brushes up behind me.

At first I think she is just getting pushed into me by the Ving Rhames-type dude behind her, and I feel bad, bad that I cannot get my Ving to move, and bad that she does not have enough room.

Then she starts to speak, and when she does I stop

feeling so bad.

"What's wrong with people," she says, clearly talking to me, about me and through me. "They don't fucking move for anybody, they just stand there, not moving, not trying to move, not a care in the world."

My guilt becomes exasperation.

I turn to face her, motion to the behemoth in front of me, and give her a look that I hope says, "Gimme a break, what am I supposed to do here?"

She has no love for me though, no understanding and no lack of feelings about this predicament we are in.

"Fuck, fuck, fuck, fuck, motherfucker, fuck, fuck, fuck, fuck," she says.

Well, she may not be saying exactly that, but it certainly sounds a lot like it.

This goes on for several minutes, no one seeming to notice or care, least of all Ving.

"Fuck, fuck, fuck, fuck, motherfucker, fuck, fuck, fuck, fuck," she continues.

I finally look at her and say, "And what the fuck would you have me do?"

There is a pause, and then her Ving leans over, stares at me and says somewhat menacingly, "Now, why don't you show the lady some respect."

I do not respond.

Instead, I turn away, face my Ving's back and find a

happy place to focus on until my stop comes up.

I'm tired.

Not tired of New York City or the subway of course, I love them both, but I am definitely tired, very, very tired.

Tired of my inability to help the children and families that I work with.

Tired of the shell-shocked neighbor and his angry pit bull that we constantly need to avoid in the halls of our apartment building.

Tired of watching John Starks miss three-pointers.

And tired of the endless stream of cockroaches that inhabit our wannabe one bedroom apartment, despite all our best efforts to stop them, including our use of the magic chalk from Chinatown that helps some, but not enough.

And then there I am on the N train, minding my own business, reading my *Newsday*, and heading to visit someone.

It's hot and I'm tired, which you know, and he walks up.

He's a pasty white guy, with long brown hair and a beard.

He's wearing several layers of mismatched clothes.

He's clearly homeless.

He stops right in front of where I am sitting, the fluorescent lights washing over him and setting off a weird glow.

He doesn't say a word to me.

He just stands there and stares.

I look up over the top of my newspaper and we make eye contact, but he still doesn't say a word.

I look back down, but he doesn't go away.

Nor does he say anything.

He's just standing, not talking, not moving.

A minute passes, and then another, nothing, no movement, no words, nothing.

I look up again. Should I say something? And if so, what should I say?

He must want money, right?

But he hasn't said so, and I don't have any, I really don't, I never carry any with me.

If he doesn't want money why else is he standing there?

Might he be a messenger of some kind from the other side?

Maybe this is like an episode of *The Twilight Zone*. Maybe he's me from the future or in a parallel world? Maybe the universe has inverted itself while I've been underground and everyone is now homeless but me? Then again, who's to say I'm not homeless too?

He still hasn't said a word.

Now I feel angry.

Is he trying to intimidate me or stage some kind of silent protest against all that I represent?

"Hey man," I say to him, "I'm a social worker. I'm on your side, go pick on one of the lawyers on the other end of the car."

Okay, I don't say that, but I do speak to him.

"Hey man," I say, "what do you want from me?"

He doesn't speak at first, but then says, "I need some money to eat."

"I don't have it brother, I'm sorry," I say.

"I said, I need some money for food," he says raising his voice and stepping closer to me.

"I really don't have any," I say.

"I said, I need some money for food," he repeats.

"Hey man," I say starting to feel little waves of panic crawl up my neck, and wondering if I can get around him if needed, "do you want one of my sandwiches, I brought two for lunch."

He mulls this over, not saying a word.

"You said you wanted some food, right," I say my voice raising, "and now I'm offering you some, do you want it or not? And if you don't please move the fuck away from me."

"Okay, sure," he says.

I hand him a sandwich wrapped in aluminum foil and he opens it up.

He looks unhappy.

"Peanut butter and jelly," he says disgustedly, "is that all you have?"

"Look buddy," I say, "if you don't want it give it back, that's my lunch."

"No man, I'll eat it," he says.

He walks away.

I get off the train a few stops later, and now I'm really tired.

SPLIT SCREEN

We are hunkered down around the little white television we used to have.

The television was my then girlfriend Debbie's when we were in college, and it fits our current surroundings: a somewhat dingy, much too small, yet hoping to be more, one-bedroom apartment, that is really just a studio with a wall.

It is June 17, 1994.

We are watching Game 5 of the NBA Finals, the Knicks are playing the Rockets at the Garden, and we are hoping to watch them go up 3-2 in the series.

We want this win, we are focused on the game before us and we are not moving.

The Knicks deserve our full attention and they must have it.

This is their night.

This is our night.

And we are taking no chances that we will inadvertently cause the Knicks to lose by getting distracted and not providing them with the proper dosage of the energy, positive Karma, and undiluted attention that only we can provide.

Their win depends on our ability to will it into being so, hence there will be no distractions, just hunker.

But then the chase happens.

Soon NBC is switching between the game and the L.A. Freeway, then they move to a split screen, and ultimately we are forced to do everything in our power to give the Knicks what they need, despite our inability to pretend in this moment that they are all we care about.

We live on 96th Street, off of West End, and we are just an overpass away from the West End Highway. We do not cross under the overpass at night because we are convinced that trolls live under it.

Not that the neighborhood doesn't basically feel safe if you ignore the crack den on 95th and focus on the parking garage across the street from our building. The garage is open 24-hours a day, which means lots of light and security throughout the night, something considered an amenity in the housing market at the time.

There is our shell-shocked neighbor though, the one who keeps the mouth of his feral pit bull taped shut with duct tape, is rumored to walk the halls at night with a hunting knife, and just weeks after the game will blow-up his apartment one beautiful Sunday afternoon.

And yet, we don't remotely believe that our somewhat sketchy living conditions have any greater importance or bearing than most anyone else's living in New York City at the time.

It is the early 1990's and there is a lot of shit going on.

There is the first World Trade Center bombing in February of 1993, when a truck loaded with explosives is parked under the North tower for what turns out to be a test run.

There is Joel Rifkin's arrest in June of 1993 for murdering sixteen women over a four year span and leaving their bodies to decompose in the wilds of Long Island.

There is the Long Island Railroad massacre in December 1993, when Colin Ferguson shoots and kills six passengers, while wounding nineteen others.

There is my co-worker's sexual assault on a suddenly empty train passing under the East River, as well as, my own physical assault which I suffer just two months before the game on 125th street one sunny evening after work as I walk to Ben & Jerry's for a milk shake.

And maybe this is as it always is, just merely something

new to me, and those whom I grew-up with, striving middle-class Americans from small towns, born of a privilege that comes with being white, and in my case male, who have not grown-up in violent homes or violent neighborhoods, and so have not known day to day violence, much less the tension of managing the fear that comes with it.

None of which should ignore the pleasures that also existed in early 1990's New York: the late night clubs such as Webster Hall and the Tunnel where we munched hallucinogens and danced until daybreak, before stopping in the Meat Packing district at Le Florent to have breakfast on the way home; drinking in Max Fish's Café and McSorley's in Alphabet City and the lower East Side, respectively; listening to David Murray at the Village Vanguard and the Wrench at CBGB's; seeing the debuts of plays such as *Oleanna* by David Mamet in the East Village and *Angels in America* by Tony Kushner and *Two Trains Running* by August Wilson during their opening run on Broadway; and buying bagels so hot at H&H Bagels on Broadway while walking home in the middle of the night, that they verged on melting in our bare hands.

All of that, and watching our beloved Knicks of course, including, but not limited to, Charles Oakley, John Starks, the recently departed Anthony Mason, and my great love, Patrick Ewing.

All of which is to say, that it was a vibrant, scary, amazing time, and the city badly wanted, if not outright needed this win over the Rockets, and this despite the fact that the Rangers had won the Stanley Cup earlier that week after 54 years of yearning.

Then again, maybe none of this true.

Maybe that's how I remember it, and maybe that was me projecting my needs and fears and confusion onto the city itself, a city I had adopted as my own, and loved, but hadn't found as welcoming as I assumed it would be.

All of which is also to say that maybe this is less a story about New York in the 1990's, and more a story about what New York meant to me at the time.

I had idolized Patrick Ewing since the moment that I stumbled onto a photo of him in *Sport* magazine cradling a ball near his head and stating, "I take it personally when you come into my neighborhood."

It was his unabashed mix of ferocity and pride; the power game mixed with the light touch around the basket; the anger and smile; the grace he showed when subjected to the terrible, racist things people felt they had permission to say about him because he was a public figure, because he was a big man fighting big men when it was still a big man's game, and because of his looks—too black, too African, too something.

On a more base level though, I loved him because he was tough and cool, and I wanted to be tough and cool.

As a teenager I never felt tough or cool enough, something that had seemingly, or mostly passed, but here, now, in the New York City of the early 1990's, I suddenly felt that way again.

Prior to this, I had been living in San Francisco, playing ultimate Frisbee, and going to Dead shows, and my stoner humor had fit right in there.

But I was suddenly out of sorts again.

I wanted to fit in, and build some kind of community, but I couldn't find a new ultimate Frisbee team to play on, and I couldn't quite figure out how to build anything else to fill that void.

There had also been the aforementioned assault, which left me feeling vulnerable and exposed, and not the kind of man I thought I was or should be.

There was Patrick Ewing though, on the screen, bigger than life, and as tough and cool as ever, as well as the Knicks, and while we knew that they were counting on our role alone in ensuring that night's win, there was a still a sense of community that surrounded the team, the season, this series, and especially this game, that I needed and they were only too happy to provide.

So there we were in the NBA Finals with Ewing, despite

his greatness, clearly overmatched against the Rockets' Hakeem "The Dream" Olajuwon, he of the grace and quick feet, shot making prowess, ease around the basket and all-around big man dominance.

We, he, Patrick Ewing would have to be greater than great to beat Hakeem, and no, basketball is not a one man game, and there would have been no 2-2 tie going into Game Five without Starks and Mase and Oakley, but it was Ewing's moment, and if he could not be transcendent in the way the greatest athletes can be, he had to at least be Hakeem's equal.

Ewing did his part, mostly, with a record 30 blocks in the series, and a ridiculous Game 5 given his match-up against the Dream:

21 points.

12 rebounds.

8 blocks.

And yet, today, do we truly remember Ewing's brilliance in the game?

A game in which the Knicks went up 3-2, needing only one more win in the final two, albeit in Houston, to clinch the title?

We do not, not really, and we do not because of that super slow chase along the L.A. Freeway, the white Bronco and O.J. Simpson.

O.J. Simpson who won the Heisman Trophy and then

went on to become the first NFL running back to run for over 2000 yards in a season.

O.J. Simpson who, for a stretch of entertainment history, crossed all sorts of pop culture and racial lines by playing a Conehead on *Saturday Night Live,* running through airports in Hertz commercials, acting opposite Leslie Nielsen in *The Naked Gun* movies and starring in *Roots.*

O.J. Simpson who was rejected for Arnold Schwarzenegger's role in *The Terminator* because James Cameron did not think he would be believable as a killer.

O.J. Simpson who was now accused of brutally murdering his wife Nicole Brown Simpson and her friend Ron Goldman.

And what could be more Icarus-like than all that?

Nothing, not really, and not in the stark terms that were wrapping themselves around this story—the greatest heights and glory, the near-mythic storyline of "The Juice," all undone, by hubris certainly, but something else as well, weakness, violence and the idea that women serve at the pleasures of men.

Until they don't, or in this case, refuse to.

And now this, the police had been dispatched to O.J.'s home that day to bring him in. He had in turn slipped away with his life-long friend AC Cowlings in a white Ford Bronco and was soon leading the LAPD on a really slow chase along the L.A. Freeway, NBC at first switching between the game and the chase, before eventually moving to a split screen and showing both at the same time.

As it was, we were already breathless, living and dying, with every basket the Knicks made, and did not, and before the split screen, every time NBC switched away from the game.

But we were also breathless as we watched a sports and pop culture icon we all worshipped, or once had anyway, on the run, wondering how it would all end.

Now, was it true to say that the March 1991 beating of Rodney King by the Los Angeles Police Department, and the subsequent acquittal of the police officers in April and May 1992 hovered over the proceedings just as the omnipresent helicopters were doing throughout the chase?

Of course it was.

So, did we want O.J. to escape then?

Yes, we did, sort of.

Did we want a shoot-out?

Maybe, no, probably not, but we wondered what it would look like.

Did we want O.J. to kill himself?

No, not really, though we wondered about that too, because how *wasn't* it going to end like that?

It was possible that O.J. would escape to Mexico of course, and we all kind of wanted that too, or the idea of it, anyway.

It was the most fantastical, and impossible, outcome imaginable, and yet, why wasn't it within the realm of possibility that O.J. could elude the police in the same fashion he once had the tacklers so set on bringing him down to earth among the rest of the us?

It was totally possible.

It was also spectacle; both reality television before there was quite such a thing outside of *Real World*, and a media frenzy that was a real time life and death race against time—the news cameras were everywhere, and we did not know what would happen next, any more than we now know how a leg of the *Amazing Race* will end.

We just know it will end, eventually, and so we keep watching.

What does it say about us that we could not look away though, and that in so many ways, we were ready to watch someone die, live and televised?

Or that we really didn't know, or care, where O.J. had been or what he was doing for some time now, and that before all of this we were essentially done with him, as we would soon be with Patrick Ewing?

That we use heroes until they are no longer useful for us, and then we let them drift away to figure out on their own what comes after the lights and the adulation are gone?

How about the fact that many of us are white and

that we worship black males, but otherwise treat them as disposable, and the other, here for our entertainment, but nothing more?

Because all of that was at play during these hours, life and death, game and chase, race and privilege, and yet what does it also mean, that even though a man's life was at stake, it was no more important to us than this game, and the gift that Patrick Ewing was simultaneously delivering to us, his delirious fans?

And what about the fact that O.J. ultimately gave up, peacefully, parked his car and left with the police?

Was that truly the end we wanted?

Do we even know?

Also, what does it mean that the Knicks would go on to lose Games 6 and 7, the former by a sliver, as the Dream blocked Starks' shot in the closing seconds—following a lights out shooting performance in the fourth quarter—and the latter a showcase for an Icarus-light implosion by Starks as he tragically fell back to the court after scaling such great heights?

How did we feel about that, though more importantly, how could we also feel like that was a death, when there was so much actual death in the air?

Because we needed it.

We need heroes, and we need community, and we need to believe, that these things are real, because if they're not, what else is there besides real life in all of its ugliness?

I moved to Chicago shortly after Game 7 to go to graduate school, Michael Jordan came out of retirement, and I had to watch the Knicks lose again and again at his hand, and nowhere closer to a title, except for a blow-out loss to the Spurs in the finals years later as Ewing sat on the bench, injured, impotent, and not long for New York, or any of his former glory.

One afternoon I left school and walked to Jimmy's Woodlawn Tavern and stood around in the crowd of academics and construction workers, a low buzz electrifying the room, as we huddled around the little television above the bar and watched as O.J. Simpson was acquitted for the double-homicide he had been charged with.

At first there was a stunned silence, and then applause, before the crowd slowly moved back onto the street.

Something had happened, but the significance of what it was, was not quite clear, and may not be yet, except for the feeling that we were at the precipice of a new era, a period when the real time emergence of the internet, social media, and 24-hour coverage of anything, and all things, celebrity and scandal, would be ascendant, and we would soon find ourselves speeding into a world where no secrets were safe, and no stories would be buried, not for long, certainly.

And while quickly enough there was all of that, there was also a re-definition of what heroes might be, because in a world where heroes may still get a pass for their most aberrant behavior, we now know everything, believe we should know everything, and regularly learn, that much of it isn't very pretty at all, much less heroic.

APARTMENT LIVING

I am leaving San Francisco.

It's been a good run, full of Grateful Dead shows, ultimate Frisbee, the House of Nanking and unicorn acid tabs.

But I am done being so far away from my family and my girlfriend Debbie. I head to New York City and for the first several months I am in town I crash on the living room floor of my friends, Avi and Ira.

We smoke a lot of pot, and watch a lot of Knicks' games, and while they never ask anything of me and would probably never ask me to leave, my freeloading starts to feel awkward after awhile.

I sublet half of a basement apartment in a duplex on 26th Street in Chelsea and I share the basement with a guy named Keith. My space is separated from the rest of the apartment by a sheet stretched across the common room, while Keith has an actual bedroom.

Keith is blonde and handsome in a Culkin kind of way. He spends most of his time working on a movie script that has something to do with an international blood smuggling cartel. Keith rarely moves and only leaves the basement once a day to buy Snapple lemonade.

The upstairs floor in the duplex is inhabited by a waitress named Stacey. She is really nice, though never around, which is good, because the mole on her chin is so large, hence so distracting to me, that I rarely remember anything we've talked about when we're done doing so.

When my sublet is up Debbie and I go look for a place where we can move in together.

Everything we can afford is small, dirty, and expensive, and we settle on a place on the upper West side.

It is advertised as a one-bedroom apartment, but in reality it's a studio apartment where someone has thrown up a wall to create a small bedroom, leaving the kitchen in the now quasi-separate living room.

The entire apartment would fit in the combined dining and living rooms of the apartment I left in San Francisco.

The apartment is located by the underpass at 96th and the Hudson River Parkway, which we will avoid using at night after we become convinced that trolls live there and are waiting to murder us.

I should add that we were quite high, quite often back then.

The apartment is also across the street from a 24-hour parking garage, which we are told is a benefit because between the lights and the staff, it's like having a bonus security system built into the neighborhood.

I'm not sure about all of that, but late one night the lights will certainly serve to enhance our view as a skinny drug dealer in full sprint is tackled by a team of burly undercover cops right at our feet as we are getting home.

"By the way," Lloyd the slumlord tells us moments after we sign our lease, "the guy across the hall from you can be a little crazy. He can also be your best friend though, I do know that he helped some girls in the building set-up their shelves."

Lloyd is tall and lean with gelled salt-and-pepper hair and French cuffs.

He's too smooth by half, and he's a liar, everyone in the room knows that. Debbie and I decide to ignore this though, we are sick of looking at apartments and we don't want to fret about the neighbors.

As it turns out, the neighbor is a shell-shocked Korean War veteran who wears nothing but Army fatigues, has refused all renovations and repairs to his apartment for decades and is rumored to roam the halls at night, unspeaking, butcher knife in hand.

He is also known for walking around the neighborhood with a homicidal looking pit bull he keeps at bay with a chain.

The night we move our things into the apartment, Avi and I do bong hits for several hours before touching a single box.

As we bring the first load over from his apartment around the corner, we are laughing and stumbling, unbalanced, but joyful.

As we enter the lobby of our building we see the neighbor standing there with the pit bull by his side.

While the neighbor seems to have a firm hold on the chain, and the dog's mouth is bound shut with black electrical tape, Avi and I pause for a moment before heading into the lobby.

As we approach the neighbor, the pit bull lunges at us, its lips twisted and curling, spittle flying out from beneath the tape.

We are paralyzed with fear, but in the nanosecond it takes the dog to move, the neighbor, with a gracefulness belying his age, lifts his left knee and pins the dog's head against the wall.

"You better move on now," the neighbor says.

We do.

—

The neighbor isn't the only neighbor we meet, or more accurately, sort of meet.

There is also the shut-in down the hall that we don't know is a shut-in.

The first day we move in I need a plunger, we do not have one and knock on the shut-in's door.

"Go away," he says quietly through the closed door.

"I just need to borrow a plunger," I say.

"Go away, go away, go away," he screams through the door.

Then silence.

And then there is the avuncular young guy I meet on the elevator one day who asks me if I want to get high with him and listen to the live DOORS CD he has just purchased.

I do, a number of times, until one day he's just gone.

Years later I will run into him on a train when Debbie and I are back in New York City for my bachelor party.

He is as friendly as he ever was and we pick-up as if no time has passed at all "How's the girlfriend, brother?" he asks.

"Good," I reply, "we're getting married next month, you?"

"Great, I just got out of prison in Thailand," he says with a smile.

"Yeah?"

"Yeah, smuggling drugs."

"Great, welcome back."

Meanwhile, the neighbor lurks around corners and in the aisles of the Big Apple supermarket up the street from our building.

He is the scariest person we have ever seen.

Debbie asks me to speak to Lloyd.

"Ask him if there are any plans to get him out of the building," she says, "and if not, why not?"

I don't want to speak to Lloyd, not about this, nor anything else, but I am the man of the house, and this apparently is the kind of thing the man is supposed to do.

"Hey Lloyd," I say as I find myself sitting in his office shortly thereafter, "are there any plans to try and evict the neighbor?"

"Plans," he says running his hand through his salt and pepper hair, "I've been trying to get rid of him for years. He came with the building. Do you know how cheap he's getting that place? I can't get rid of him, he has to do something first. You help me out here however, and we all win."

"Sure man," I say.

Debbie and I resign ourselves to the cards we have been

dealt.

The neighbor is not going anywhere and there isn't anything we can do about it.

We avoid him as much as possible, which isn't hard really because we quickly learn to never stop and speak to anyone, much less dawdle, when we leave or enter our apartment.

One Palm Sunday the neighbor leaves the city for the day to attend a funeral. He locks the pit bull in his closet and lines his windows with exposed wire, so that anyone who tries to break into his apartment will be electrocuted.

The wire shorts, there is an explosion and his apartment goes up in flames.

Debbie and I are not home for the explosion, but we return to our apartment as the firemen are finishing their work.

They have put out the fire and saved the dog, though one of the firemen has been bit while doing so.

The dog is placed with the Red Cross and the firemen leave a note for the neighbor about where he can find both the dog and emergency shelter.

The neighbor returns home later that night—and long after we've gone to bed—and Debbie and I are awakened by the subsequent shouting.

"Where's my dog," the neighbor screams over and over again to no one in particular.

We lay in bed too petrified to move.

We hear a crash, and then another.

There is banging, and rattling.

The noise grows louder and closer.

We hear the neighbor panting outside our door.

Debbie begs me to go look out the peephole.

My vision is limited and warped. I can see what's in front of me, but only slightly to the right or left.

The neighbor's door is wide open and blackened with soot, nothing is happening right in front of our apartment, and the neighbor is nowhere to be seen.

To my left though is an incredible sight—a wet, black, congealed mass of televisions, toaster ovens, space heaters, furniture, microwaves and coffee pots so great that it has filled the garbage room next to our apartment and like the illustration for a Shel Silverstein fire prevention poem is now overflowing out of the garbage room door, climbing up towards the ceiling and edging its way across the hall and into the neighbor's apartment.

We don't sleep at all the rest of the night, lying there instead, staring at the ceiling, bathed in the oozy lights of the parking garage across the street.

When Debbie and I prepare to leave for work the next morning our challenge is obvious—to reach the elevator or stairwell we are going to need to slide around the burnt appliance mountain directly in front of the neighbor's still open door, not knowing whether he is waiting there for us or not.

We wait as long as we can to make our move, and then like commandos plot our escape.

I will go first with Debbie just steps behind me in case the neighbor awaits us with a knife. If I am stabbed Debbie will head back into the apartment to protect herself with me in close pursuit.

She is on strict orders, however, to leave me behind if I cannot retreat.

At that point I will either fight the neighbor to death, or more ideally make a move to the stairwell.

As it turns out though, the neighbor is gone and we are safe to escape into the bright morning sun.

That afternoon when I return home from work I see the neighbor out in front of our building talking with the police.

I wonder whether I should turn around before he sees me, but it's too late.

"That's him, that's the guy," he screams at the police, "the professor, he set the fire."

The police ignore him, look at me shaking their heads and wave me into the building.

Lloyd calls me later that week.

"How would you feel about testifying against the neighbor," he says, "this is our chance to get him."

Lloyd is being very friendly. Suddenly, we're buddies, compadres.

"I don't know Lloyd," I say.

Helping out Lloyd is not so appealing to me. I'm not only scared of the neighbor, but I feel empathy for him now as well—he has already lost his home, he is a war veteran, and he is sick, need we add insult to injury?

On top of that, Debbie and I are getting ready to move and as we plan to stick Lloyd with the security for our last month's rent, I want to keep all contact with him to a minimum.

"C'mon," he says, "don't you want to see him go?"

"I guess, sure," I say, "but where will he live?"

"He's got a daughter he's staying with," Lloyd says. "He's fine."

"Let me think about it," I reply.

"Sure," Lloyd says, with a resignation I know well.

I don't speak to Lloyd after that, nor do I never see the neighbor again.

A month later, someone sets the interior of the elevator on fire, and while they never catch the perpetrator many people in the building are sure they saw the neighbor leaving that day.

Debbie and I move out several weeks after that, and a brief stop in the East Village, we head to Chicago, where a new life and new neighbors await us.

DRINKING: A LOVE STORY

Like so many nights, it begins with a drink. And like so many others it ends on a cold bathroom floor, half-dressed, the rank smell of vomit in the air.

The scene is one of those early 1990's New York City clubs that was so of the moment, and so hip, that weeks before we probably couldn't even have gotten in.

You know those bars—dark, loud, and lots of metal, mostly brushed, smoke for sure and maybe some bubbles. The halls all narrow and crowded, and the bathrooms tiny, the stalls filled with people doing blow or getting blown.

There are two kinds of patrons here. There are the suits, those who are wearing Armani, the hair slicked back or playfully tussled, and the vampires, the patrons with the long gaunt faces, who are clad in jeans and black T-shirts, black, the occasional white T-shirt thrown in for the sake of variety.

And then there's us, Debbie and me, and I'm not even sure what we're doing in a club like this. It's not that we don't belong here per se, we're young and attractive and all, it's just that I'm not sure we even know where to start. There are rules here and norms in clubs like this, certain drinks to order and a certain kind of banter, and I don't know that we know these things.

I do know though that they need us here—because there are a dozen clubs out there ready to take their place—and that we need them—if for any other reason, so that we can say we've been here, if not now, then ten years from now, when we are older and lamer, and laughing about the places we once went, the people we once were.

I also know that we know how to drink, a skill that transcends all clubs, cities, and genders. If you can hold your own, you will be down anywhere, with any one, at least for that moment, and we can definitely hold our own.

We order Kamikazes, a drink I've never been a big fan of. At best they seem like chick drinks, like a Sex on the Beach or a Buttery Nipple, and at worst they are a thick, syrupy mess of a drink that coats your tongue like enamel.

But there we are and Kamikazes seem to be the drink of choice, so we order not one, but two rounds each, because it's late, because we're too drunk to know better, and because we still like to believe that a table full of empty shot glasses somehow looks cool.

The shots arrive—doubles—and the drinks are so cloudy I can see my reflection morph ghost-like and blurry on the side of the glass as I raise it to my lips.

They go down quickly, though not quickly enough, and as we stare at the empty glasses before us we realize that we are now officially too drunk to talk, but not yet drunk enough to head home.

Someone decides that it may just be best if we dance, and looking back I think we can now clearly identify that moment as the point of no return.

Wallowing in a drunken stupor is something most any drinker can do for any number of hours as needed.

It's not like drinking has anything to do with needing to think or concentrate or anything like that—if anything we drink because we prefer not to think, too much pain or confusion or whatever forever lurking on the edges of sobriety.

But getting up to dance in such a condition is another story of course, because that requires a set of skills, balance for example, that we can only hope to embrace for a couple of minutes at best.

Tonight is no exception.

Debbie is soon hugging, and then sliding down the wall in the back, and it's not that she isn't as lovely as ever. Her long brown hair draped over her kick ass clavicles; her smile, even in this state, vibrant and paralyzing; her skin, luminous, like fresh fruit, is as aglow as the first time I met her.

Her long shapely legs however, while killer as ever, are buckling beneath her, and she's definitely morphing herself from beautiful woman to beautiful puddle.

It is time to go.

We find a cab and head south down Broadway, past Union Square Park, and the desperate, too many to ignore homeless men that sleep there. As Debbie slumps on my shoulder, I see them through a drunken haze, sleeping under shopping carts and huddling around small bonfires. This image continues to haunt me as we pull up to the apartment we are crashing in, and I try to figure out when and how we became pseudo, wanna-be, IKEA-buying, Banana Republic wearing, Kamikaze drinking yuppie scum.

We had launched our relationship in the dank and dirty bars of upstate New York, eating Slim Jims, drinking too much Vodka and looking to one another to fix our broken parts.

Somewhere along the way though we had grown-up, or worse maybe, just got older, and now here we were, but one day away from packing our bags and moving to Chicago, stumbling through the East Village, fumbling with our keys and staring at four flights of warped stairs in the pre-war walk-up we were temporarily calling home.

I wonder what this big move means for us and where we are going, and I think about how great it would be to see a sign, some really obvious *L.A. Story* on the side of the highway kind of sign, telling me that we are in a new place now, that I can trust it, and that I need to run with it.

We have just reached our floor when Debbie tells me that she thinks she is going to throw-up.

Everyone who drinks knows at least one fellow drinker who prides themselves on never having thrown-up and Debbie has always been that person for me.

There is a first time for everything though, and so I walk her to the bathroom as she has done for me so many times before and help her kneel in front of the toilet.

It isn't pretty—of course—it never is, but I pull her hair back from her face and brush her teeth, and these are things I am only too happy to do.

What I am not happy to do, however, is acquiesce to the request that follows shortly thereafter.

"I want to sleep right here on the floor," she says.

"What?"

"I want sleep right here, in the bathroom, it's safer."

"Why?"

"What if I get sick again?"

"I'll bring a garbage can into bed with us," I say in a quite reasonable tone.

"No, I want to sleep here."

Arguing is clearly fruitless at this point, but I keep trying anyway, and more desperately, at that.

"But it's really fucking cold in here."

"So get a blanket," she says.

"And these old tiles, while stylish certainly, are really fucking hard," I reply.

"And pillows," she adds.

"And I have no choice do I?" I say losing any hope of this happening, and by this, I mean sleeping in a warm bed.

"Not if you love me," she says.

Fuck, it's hard to argue with that, especially at four in the morning.

So, I get some pillows and a blanket and tuck us in, and despite the cold tiles, and the fact that there is barely space on the floor for two to begin with, I find myself thinking about love, and the first time we kissed—in a bar, no less—and as I start to lose myself in this reverie, Debbie speaks one more time.

"I'm done drinking, I mean it, this is it," she says before drifting off.

I know she means it, because while most drinkers say this at one time or another, and then start right back-up again, Debbie is different. When she says she's done with something she usually is. So forget the reveries, because now as I drift off I have drinking on my mind, or not drinking, and what that all means to me and us.

While I have always gravitated towards the drinkers in any crowd, I had also always wanted something more for myself, and by extension, us—a deeper, richer, more conscious way of being, and if she, and by extension we, are not going to being drinking anymore, at least not together, might not those kinds of things be possible then?

All of that is a lot to sleep on, but sleep I do, and well, until I start feeling a cold that is like so cold, that it is an, *I can feel the tiles through the blanket and pillows kind of cold*.

I wonder if I'm dreaming, but no I'm not dreaming at all, because as it turns out I'm lying there on the bathroom floor all by myself, no pillows, no blanket, no Debbie—she has gone off to bed without me.

I'm too cold to even move immediately, and so I wrap myself in the hand towel I have grabbed for warmth and I begin to think again about all this change that's happening, and how this little window has opened up for me, and us, how here we were already making this move, which is so big any way, and now there's the whole not drinking thing, and it all seems so promising, maybe.

I start to feel real excitement about all of it, and I start to think about how I need to find a way to signify just how big all this is, and that's when it strikes me—it's really so obvious—it's time to propose.

This thinking may be a result of the cold swelling my brain or the hangover clouding my thinking, but love is in the air, and change is afoot—I'm sure of that—and I know I need to do something special.

I also know that I need to do it now while the opportunity is staring me in the face because what if it somehow passes me, and us, by?

I'm not going to take that chance, and at this point the adrenaline starts pumping, and yes, this decision is a scary one, but it seems so right in that moment, and so pure that I want to scream from the rooftops, "Yo, New York City, I'm going to propose."

I don't actually do this of course, because if I were to, someone would tell me just to jump already, and someone else would to tell me to shut the hell up because they're sleeping and most everyone else would say that they don't give a rat's ass whether I have made such a monumental decision or not because to be frank it isn't so fucking monumental to them—they have bills to pay and sick kids and heroin habits and soaps to watch and lives of their own.

All of which, may merely be a comment on the breakdown of community, and an example of the small, but significant ways we no longer take an interest in our neighbors. Then again this is New York City we are talking about, not Des Moines, and so maybe it isn't that big a deal any way you spin it.

Plus, while I could dissect, analyze, and examine this issue to death, the sun is coming up and I'm just wasting valuable time at this point if I do.

So, there I am, a man with a plan, kind of anyway. Making the decision to propose is great and all, but then reality hits. I'm leaving town and while I can wait to propose until we were on the road, I have to have something to propose with, right?

Right, but it isn't like I am going to go out and buy Debbie an actual engagement ring on my own.

There is just no way I am going to get that right.

I can get something temporary though, a ring that says, *"Hey, I'm lovely and special and kind of magical and here to tide you over until you and Ben make the time to come back to town and head down to the diamond district."*

Of course, now I have to find such a ring and I only have like three hours.

But I am down in the Village and how hard can it be to find something like that in the Village?

I'm guessing not so hard, and so out I go, reeking of alcohol certainly, but with a little hop in my step, none-the-less.

I head south on Broadway and I am immediately taken with the East Village in the not-quite-so-early late morning.

The air is moist, the sun is just starting to break and things are already jumping as I roll by Astor Place.

There are the Rastas putting out their essential oils,

their long dreadlocks all bunched up on top of their heads and the Pakistani guys tucked into their breakfast carts, dispensing fried egg sandwiches, coffee and chocolate doughnuts.

There are the scruffy leather jacketed guys unpacking their Dead bootlegs and the hip-hop boys from Queens with their techno inspired mixed tapes.

And then there are the African guys selling their sunglasses and the dudes from the Middle East pushing cell phones and beepers.

It's all hustle and bustle down there and awfully exciting for a guy on a mission, kind of like watching the circus set up when it first rolls into town.

As I continue down Broadway I find myself drawn into the Antique Boutique, if for no other reason than the fact that it's open and kind of hip, usually reasonable, and has the words antique and boutique in the title, which says to me that a passable yet tasteful ring may be in the offing.

I cruise by the all decked out in black, Ray Ban wearing guard at the door and avoid the multi-berreted, green haired, horned rimmed glasses wearing Lisa Loeb looking sales girl as well, because trying to explain to either of them what I am doing there seems too embarrassing, too unreal or too something.

After wandering hopelessly for several minutes I begin to realize that the antique in the title mainly seems to refer to the 50-year old tuxedo coats and ancient bowling shirts that appear to dominate every rack in the store.

I do eventually find a counter, however, and though initially hopeful, I quickly learn that one, 1980's-era Swatches already qualify as antiques and two, the selection of rings is limited to $500 chunky plastic pseudo diamonds that come in array of colors my grandmother wouldn't even wear.

Not quite sure what to do at this point I stare at the contents wanting to believe that if I stand there long enough the ring I seek will somehow magically appear.

It doesn't, but I do hear a voice from somewhere behind me asking me whether I am "looking for an engagement ring?"

I turn around to find this little Buddy Holly looking guy staring at me—he is clearly the long lost third member of We Might be Giants—and I tell him that yes, in fact, I am.

I want to ask him how he knows this, but I am completely flummoxed by the fact that someone in New York City would be so willing to initiate a conversation.

"You're not going to find what you're looking for here," he says, "but I have just the place for you to go."

"And where would that be?" I ask.

"You need to go to Effervescence on MacDougal, it's below Mahmoud's Felafel. You can't miss it. I've shot some stuff there," he says, "and they will have you what need, I promise."

"Sounds good to me," I reply. "Who should I say sent me?"

"Tell them Dr. Feelgood sent you."

Of course.

With that he's gone, lost in the swirl of polyester shirts, and shortly after that I'm gone as well, heading west across town and wondering whether if this encounter actually just happened, and if so, whether it is a sign of some sort or just another random exchange in a day that may prove to be full of them.

Along the way, I find myself cruising by NYU and its lovely denim covered, baseball hat wearing co-eds, and then past Washington Square Park, which is overrun with skateboard punks in long t-shirts, knit caps, baggy shorts and surly attitudes, something that no doubt thrills Larry Clark to no end.

I next run into an endless row of booksellers showing their wares, new books and old, all the *Vanity Fairs* and *People* magazines you could want and an amazingly dog-eared copy of *Travels with Charlie* by John Steinbeck that I decide I must have.

And then I'm on MacDougal, and while I have been there so many times before, and have even eaten at Mahmoud's, I just can't remember ever seeing a store where engagement rings might be sold.

But when I get there, I see that there is a dark stairway there, and that the stairway actually leads to a small door, and that on that door is a little sign that reads Effervescence, and I wonder if somehow this store has been put here at this time and in this place just for me.

I'm nervous to go in, but know I must, and like Alice, I'm kind of curious too, and that curiosity gets the best of me, and I just kind of plunge through the door.

When I get inside I am struck by just how light and dark a place can be all at once.

On the one hand the store is absolutely cave-like and from the vantage point of the entrance it doesn't seem like it could possibly be more than five feet wide or long.

It's like walking into a closet really.

But then again it's not.

Because everywhere I look are shelves, and more shelves and then more shelves on top of those, and it's all so very bright because on those shelves are rings, thousands of them, millions maybe.

There are all kinds, platinum and plastic, silver and gold, steel and maybe even bronze for all I know, and they come in all kinds of shapes, circular of course, but square and triangular as well, and they're in all sorts of patterns, checkerboard, and roses, and barbed wire, and just about anything else one can imagine.

Then there are the stones.

There are diamonds of all sizes certainly, but pearls and rubies and emeralds, and they all shine and glisten, reflecting the light in every possible direction.

The shop in fact feels like it's pulsating, breathing even, and the glow is practically blinding.

I walk forward almost gingerly, as if the whole shop will come crashing down around me, or worse just disappear before I have a chance to make a decision.

It's much like being in a candy store—there's just so much to look at and choose from—and I'm so over stimulated that I know not where or how to even start.

And so I just push my way into the light and dark, waiting for the perfect ring to appear, which of course it does, straight ahead of me, eye-level and on a shelf on the far end of the store.

It's a dark ruby in an antique setting, clearly placed there for my convenience, and it is beckoning me—buy me, take me home, do it now, your work here is done.

And my work is done, and I go to take it and make it mine and I'm so lost in the moment, until I'm not, because as I go to grab that ring it finally hits me that I am not alone in this shop.

In fact just off to the left of the shelf is a door that leads to a small backroom, and in that room is a workbench and tools and a young guy polishing a ring—and this guy is right out of central casting. His hair is shaved close to the side of his head and somewhat spiky on top. He has just the lightest trace of a goatee, coifed just right so as to accentuate his Depp-like cheekbones and jaw line. He is wearing black jeans; high top black Doc Marten boots; and a black leather vest over a white tanktop, an outfit which allows his sculpted and tattooed arms both freedom of movement and maximum exposure.

As I stare at him he tosses a bemused look my way before refocusing on the work at hand.

Embarrassed, my attention quickly shifts back to ring, and as I turn to it I hear someone say, "So, what can we do ya for?"

It is this point that I look to my right and notice that this place not only has a workshop, but a counter and a cash register as well, not to mention autographed pictures tucked everywhere, and from everyone, Madonna, Joey Buttafeucco and Howard Stern to name just a few of the celebrities who have graced Effervescence with their presence.

There is also a small gnome-like man sitting in the corner behind the counter who has apparently been there the whole time.

"I'm looking for an engagement ring, of sorts," I say. "Dr. Feelgood sent me."

"Of course he did," the gnome says, "do you want that

ring you've been eyeing or what?"

"I think I do," but then noticing just the smallest touch of anxiety creeping up I say, "what if my girlfriend doesn't like it though, what then?"

"What then," he replies, "then you don't marry her."

"Is it really that simple?" I ask.

"Yeah," he says, "it really is."

And I believe him, I really do, and so I buy the ring, and it is right, and some time later, after the bags have been packed, and after we have driven long into the night, there will be a proposal, not to mention laughs, and tears, and even a wedding.

But that's a whole other story.

RAGE

I am on 125th Street in Harlem and it is the first nice day of spring.

The sun is creeping out from behind the clouds and the sky is fucking brilliant.

The snow is pretty much all gone, the once buried garbage all that remains from the winter months.

The vendors are back out as well. You got one guy selling essential oils and another dude moving cell phones. There are mixed tapes ranging from house music to disco. Bootleg videos. You can also get African statues. Socks—three pairs for five dollars, any number of colors and styles available. And as always, yet to be released books, still wrapped in plastic and apparently right from the truck, even if you don't know where that truck was heading or how the books ended-up on the street long before arriving in the bookstores that are supposed to be carrying them.

Meanwhile, I'm king of the fucking world.

I have completed my last home visit of the week and now I am just walking along, soaking up the city, and wondering whether I should stop and pick up a milkshake at Ben & Jerry's or just head right home for a nap.

Which is all I have to worry about, that's it, until it isn't.

As a caseworker working in kinship foster care, the unwritten rule is that when you're done with a home visit, you always take the train closest to the home that you're visiting.

But that isn't how I operate.

Why grab the A train when I can take the 2 or 3 and get off closer to home? Plus, there is that Ben & Jerry's, it's just so very nice out, why not walk some?

All of which seems cool until someone comes up behind me, and I don't mean some other pedestrian coming down the sidewalk.

No, it feels like there is someone making a beeline for me, the late day sun extending his shadow just past mine.

I assume that whoever it is, probably just wants some change. That kind of stuff happens all day long in the city.

I expect it and even try to embrace it.

I turn to face whoever it is, and there is a guy, right there—right fucking there—and he's smiling, kind of sweetly really, and he walks right up along next to me like he has something he wants to say.

I imagine I could discourage him from doing so.

Or even try to walk away from him.

But I don't do things like that.

I figure the pitch for spare change will come and then he'll be gone, another random encounter among many that day.

He doesn't ask for change.

Instead he just matches me stride for stride, not saying a word.

He's just walking, and smiling, and then he moves closer to me.

I still don't do anything.

I just look at him.

He's not smiling any more.

He puts his arm around my shoulder. We lock eyes. He smiles again. He tries to wrap his arm around my neck. I slip away.

I should run at this point. I don't. I'm too mesmerized, too surprised and too lost in the moment.

Instead, I start to back away, cautiously, slowly, much too slowly.

Boom.

He punches me in the mouth. I taste that coppery flavor blood takes on when it first hits your tongue. I focus on it, its thickness and texture.

I close my eyes.

Everything is black and off-kilter.

I shake my head looking for light and some balance.

I try to figure what is happening and how it could be happening.

I back away even further, slowly, much too slowly.

Boom.

His next punch catches me on the tip of my nose. I see little dots and swirls of color, purple mainly. I'm stunned, frozen in place. I have become a statue.

Boom.

There is a final blow, broken glasses and an eyebrow split neatly in two.

I drop to one knee. I am a boxer listening to a ten count. I cannot rise.

I look up, but all I see is a blurry face floating somewhere above me. The whole world has grown silent and empty. No cars. No horns. No people or crowds.

It's just him, and me, and all I hear is his voice.

"Get out motherfucker, just get out."

I wonder what this means and whether there is any way to escape.

I also wonder how much worse it is going to get.

But then he is gone.

I start to wander towards the subway station and home.

Someone stops me though, and insists I sit down.

Which I do.

I am confused, and tired, so very tired.

People have begun to gather around me. They are moving at half speed.

An ambulance arrives. They want to take me to the hospital. The police, however, want to talk to me first, if I'm up to it. And I want to be up to it. I want to show them that I am cool, and composed, and that I can describe the guy.

And I do stay cool.

And I do describe him right down to his rust colored down winter coat.

And I think I know how this will all play out.

I will tell my story, and I will have to get stitched-up, again, and then maybe I will go out for some drinks and watch some ball, make some jokes, and then find some convenient reason to explain things away.

And like the times when I broke my leg or caught my hand in the land mower, I will move on.

I will not look back, because that's what I do. I'm cool. It's cool. All done.

And I try to do that, I really do. I tell all the right people—my parents, Debbie, my boss—that everything is fine, cool even, and could have been so much worse.

I go to the office on Monday against everybody's

advice, I sit at my desk and I get to work.

But fuck it if I can just sit there like nothing happened.

I cannot get the guy's grin out of my head and I cannot stop running my finger across the stitches in my eyebrow.

I don't know, maybe, just maybe, it would be different if they caught the guy.

It's possible isn't it?

The thing is, this guy is never going to get caught, and since he will never be caught, I will never get the answers I seek. I will never know if he attacked me because he was hyped up on drugs, or because I am a social worker or because I am white. I will never even know if I just happened to be in the wrong place at the wrong time. The encounter was random, violent, without explanation, and maybe all of that doesn't matter. Maybe that's me trying to intellectualize the trauma, and maybe you don't get to do that?

What's fucked up though, is that the world seems so much scarier after this.

Drunks in bars are more threatening.

Late night shadows more disconcerting.

And a day doesn't go by when I don't wonder what will happen if one of those drunks or shadows comes at me.

Will I be able to run?

Will I be hurt again?

Or, will I have to defend myself?

It's that last question I fear the most.

I'm just so fucking angry now, and it's possible of course that I was always angry, and that after all this shit I'm just no longer able to run from that anger, or keep it at arm's length.

Either way, I know that I want to hit someone, some time, somehow, and when I do, I want to feel their blood on my hands as I stand over them posturing and laughing to myself. Sometimes my imagination runs wild as the shadows pass me on the street. I picture a confrontation ensuing. Voices are raised. Threats are made. Punches are thrown. Then when all is said and done I walk away from the kill, smiling and unapologetic. I feel so terribly jacked after these moments. My heart pounding so hard it's like a Goliath fucking metronome. My breathing so heavy I have to sit down so I don't hyperventilate. It's quite thrilling really, feeling something like that, something other than anger and desperation.

But then the adrenaline fades, and all that remains is fear, and a sense of powerlessness.

I realize during these darker moments that I wouldn't feel any better even if something like this did go down. The fact is, I am off balance now, and the world is no longer a place I have any mastery over.

Later, when the Iraq War is in full-swing and the

soldiers start coming home, so many, so angry and off-balance, I will read about Post-Traumatic Stress Disorder, and it's the first time that what I feel makes any sense to me.

Having words helps, but so does having context—this is what trauma looks like, and trauma fucks you up.

In comparison to all of those soldiers, I'm lucky, and I know it, scared, all of the time, and at times, somewhat unhinged, but so very lucky.

Which leaves me where exactly?

Here, I guess, it leaves me in Chicago, and feeling threatened.

"I'm going to you fuck you up."

I hear that before I see him, but I knew exactly who it was before I even look. It's Jessie, and I have been dreading this encounter.

I have heard from a coworker that he thinks that I am interested in his girlfriend. It doesn't seem to matter to him that they are consumers at the homeless drop-in center where I now work.

She thinks that I am cute, and now we have to fight.

"I said, I'm going to fuck you up," Jessie tells me again.

"I don't know what you're talking about," I reply.

This seems like a safe answer, and unlike my previous experience in this area, I quickly try to put some real space between us as I say it. Not that this is easy when we are standing on a elevated train platform that suddenly doesn't feel much wider than a diving board.

"I'm going to beat your ass next time you mess with Connie," Jessie says.

"I'm sorry," I say again, "but I don't know what you're talking about."

I say this as calmly as possible, hoping to defuse the situation, but it doesn't seem to work, not remotely, Jessie is still coming forward. His fists are balling up. His face is growing contorted, and he is shaking, even more than me, if that is possible.

I keep backing-up hoping to find a comfort zone, but none is forthcoming, and as I run out of room I begin to wonder if the stories about the third rail are true.

And then when there are almost no steps left to take, he suddenly backs off.

Why, I don't know for sure, maybe he thinks he has made his point. Maybe he is just as nervous as I am. Maybe it's just because his train is arriving.

Whatever the reason, he turns away, but leaves me with some parting words.

"I'm watching you," he says, "and I'm going to fuck you up."

As he says this, the doors to his train open up and he is gone as quickly as he arrived. The encounter has passed uneventfully, but I can't help but think about the "what ifs."

What if I couldn't have backed away?

What if I couldn't have talked my way out of it?

What if I had been forced to do something?

I am still thinking about these things when my train comes, and I realize that bewilderment aside I'm literally shaking with anger.

I am angry that he thought it was acceptable to confront me like that and angrier still that I really didn't quite know what to do or say despite all of my fantasies about battle and revenge.

By the time I get home I have reached an all-time nadir in powerlessness and rage, that will not dissipate as it usually, eventually does.

And so I go for a run.

As I head out into the night I'm still angry.

I'm thinking about how I could just confront Jessie before he confronts me again, and that as soon as he gives me a fucked-up look, I could just sucker punch him.

As these thoughts kick in I feel my adrenaline surging and with it my running pace. As my pace picks up my form starts to get sloppy. First, my jaw tightens, and then my breathing grows irregular.

I know I need to relax and reel myself in a bit, and so I slow down, and I find myself regaining my composure, and as I do so the adrenaline begins to recede, my thoughts become less aggressive and then more clear and lucid.

Yes, I want to punch Jessie, but is that how I'm going to deal with things, much less find closure for myself, real closure?

Life is full of confrontations, big and small, and maybe I need to figure out how to better navigate those moments. Maybe I need to talk to him? It's not like everyone who confronts me is looking to draw blood.

As I continue to reframe the incident I realize that even though I initially may not have grasped it, maybe I have learned something from my previous attack besides the importance of backing the fuck up.

The fact is when Jessie confronted me I not only stayed calm, and made space for myself, but I talked my way out of a potentially precarious situation.

That's something, isn't it?

It is, because if one is not going to throw punches what more can one hope to accomplish in such a situation?

I am contemplating all this as I finish my run and as I do so I find myself moving from powerlessness to a feeling of actual empowerment.

When I was younger I would have just keep running at my sloppy, adrenaline crazed pace until I was too tired to focus on the feeling of powerlessness. When that feeling came back I would have laced up again. Hence, any feeling of power was always temporary.

But this feeling, now, this is different, this is hopeful,

and as I get home I find myself excited about going back to work the next day.

Fuck Jessie I think to myself, we're going to talk things out.

It doesn't take me long the next day to find out if I'm right.

I see Jessie almost immediately as I leave the train station. He's leaning against a building near my office. He doesn't see me coming. I walk right up to him, though I am careful not to get too close and startle him.

I also prep myself to speak calmly yet assertively—I breathe in deeply and I tell myself that this will go well, it will definitely go well.

"Jessie, what's up?" I ask.

He looks nervous and surprised to see me.

He takes a step back.

He starts wringing his hands.

He doesn't reply immediately, so I let the silence linger for a moment.

I can see that I have the upper hand.

Jessie is the one that doesn't want to be here, and he's the one that doesn't know what's going to happen.

For a moment I find myself enjoying the anxiety I see in his expressions.

I wonder what it would be like to punch him in the face.

But I will myself to relax.

I speak again trying not to sound too aggressive.

"I want to talk about what happened yesterday," I say.

"What do you mean…," he starts to say, but instead says, "I told you not to fuck with me."

I know he wants that to sound tough, but it doesn't—it comes out desperate and confused.

"I know what you told me," I reply, "but I'm not interested in Connie, I'm just trying to do my job."

"Maybe so, but how the fuck would I know that," he says. "She's always talking to you."

I weigh whether or not I should curse when answering him. With too much force it will sound confrontational, but without it I may sound weak.

So, I go for it.

"Just fucking ask me next time," I say. "That's how people work things out. And, that's how we have to work something out if you have a beef with me. Not this, you're going to kick my ass, stuff."

I know I'm pushing it, but I'm feeling more courageous now because he's not wigging out or anything.

In fact it appears like he might actually be paying attention to me.

He's looking at me in a more focused way.

His body language is relaxed.

We're almost having a conversation.

I think again about how I want to punch him, and how easily I could, but I hold back.

"Well, just watch yourself," he says, "maybe I messed-up."

I decide to push it just a little further.

"So then, we're good, right," I say.

"Yeah," Jessie replies, though not with much enthusiasm.

"No, I want to believe you," I say, "I'm not going to walk around here wondering if you're getting ready to jump me. Are we good?"

I put my hand out to shake on it.

He reaches out and says, "Yeah, fuck it, we're good."

And then, he goes his way and I go mine.

I know this is the best we're going to do. I don't know how he's feeling, but I realize that I feel pretty good.

I was scared and now I'm not.

I was angry and now I'm not.

Shit isn't always going to work out like this, but it did this time, and it is almost like a closure thing.

No, I didn't punch him in the face, but I did confront him, we reached an agreement of sorts, and it really does feel kind of empowering.

Maybe he responded as he did because he wasn't high, or because he knows he can't risk losing his services at the agency, but regardless, I can't help but smile as I walk away.

NEVER BETTER

I t was a small, but growing nonprofit in the Chicago suburbs. They had two rooms, a narrow hall, and a little office in a dusty church basement. They had recently gone from three employees to ten. Their focus was on HIV/AIDS, and while the founders had started the organization to serve their dying, white, homosexual lovers and friends, the work was changing—people of color were being infected at increasingly higher rates, as were women, and hardcore drug users.

It was the early 1990's. I was their intern. And a social work student from the University of Chicago who had been living in the mid-west for all of two weeks.

I had been chosen for this assignment because I had experience as a foster care caseworker. I had also volunteered at Gay Men's Health Crisis while living in New

York City. Still, while HIV/AIDS was an issue I felt strongly about, I knew little about the work. The public health issues of my youth had focused on wearing seatbelts and drunken driving.

I had been in a monogamous relationship for years, my biggest fear an accidental pregnancy.

I was excited to be grappling with the biggest social issue of the day, but I never believed for a moment that I knew what I was doing.

On my first day, Ken the training coordinator asked me to go to lunch.

Ken was in his sixties, he was from Kentucky and he had the sharpest teeth I had ever seen.

He told me how he had cared for hundreds of dying friends since the epidemic started, wiping their sweaty brows and offering them comfort, because that's how it was back then, people wasted away in their beds, wracked with night sweats, lesions and hallucinations, their life slowly sucked away.

It was horrible and inevitable.

I knew all of this, but Ken told me anyway, and I assumed it was a test, and a reality check, if I was going to work there, I had to be able to listen to the stories.

Then he switched gears.

"So are you gay or what?" he asked.

I paused before answering, staring at his teeth and trying to assess whether there was anything predatory about the question, and what I thought he wanted me to say.

This was the real test.

"I'm not," I said channeling Bill Murray, "but I'm willing to learn."

For a moment, Ken looked befuddled, but then he smiled and broke into laughter.

We were cool.

Among the many opportunities I was offered was taking crisis calls, something all the case managers did based on who was available when a call came in.

Some calls involved questions about benefits, and others housing, some were from people who wanted to learn more about HIV testing—where, how much, whether it was anonymous—and others from those dealing with the fall-out from their test results.

One evening I fielded one of the latter calls.

"Hello, my name is Greg, I use heroin, and I've tested positive for HIV," the guy said sounding, not a little frantic.

"All right, Greg," I said, probably sounding a little frantic myself, "you called the right place, what can I do for you?"

"I'm trying to decide whether or not to tell my girlfriend."

This was a problem.

His girlfriend was at risk, if in fact she hadn't already been exposed to the virus, and what I wanted to say was, "Are you kidding man, you haven't told her, how fucking selfish can you be?"

But I couldn't do that.

Nor could I ask him her name and tell her myself.

On the one hand, we were trained not to tell people what to do—we were there to listen, to provide support and guide them.

On the other hand, anonymity and confidentiality was valued over everything, the stigma around HIV/AIDS too great to risk exposing anyone's status.

"So why don't you want to tell her, man?" I said focusing on maintaining a neutral tone.

"Because I'm embarrassed and ashamed," he said, and I don't want to lose her. I know I should tell her though, you know? I know it's the right thing to do. I mean, you think it's the right thing to do, right?"

"What do you think, man?" I said. "It doesn't matter what I think. You said you think it's the right thing to do, and so if you believe that, you have answered the question already."

"I know, I know," he said, "and I know I should, but I can't, I want to, but I can't."

It went on like this for some time.

I listened, I gently pushed, I re-directed him, and continued to clarify what I thought he was saying, even as I was subtly trying to get him to say what I wanted him to say.

He didn't go for it though and eventually he said he had to go.

I encouraged him to call back, but he never did.

I wondered what he would do, and what was going to happen to his girlfriend.

I realized though that I would likely never learn the answers to these questions and was terribly conflicted about the choice I had made.

My supervisor Jason told me I had handled the call as I was taught, and that Greg might even call back.

My fellow students also felt I had made the right decision.

I had met the client "where he was at," that was my obligation and I had fulfilled it.

I felt sick about it though, and the call lingered on the periphery of my conscious thoughts for months afterwards, never quite going away, never quite getting resolved.

When I was still living in New York City, I went to see my doctor for routine a health exam. I hadn't had one as an adult and as the doctor went about checking me out and asking me questions he asked, "So, have you ever been tested for HIV/AIDS?"

I had not, and I was sure there was no point in doing so.

But was that absolutely the case?

I couldn't say that for sure, it was only the early 1990's and while maybe we knew everything we needed to know about HIV/AIDS, did I really trust that I knew everything I needed to know?

Not really.

I had come of age sexually as HIV/AIDS was only just piercing the collective conscious, and for the most part I had never given much thought to my own behavior or choices.

"No," I said.

"Do you want to?" he asked. "We're going to be drawing blood anyway."

"Why not," I responded.

When they took my blood they filled-up two additional test tubes of blood and as they prepared the blood to be sent out they put the two additional test tubes in a paper bag and handed them to me.

"You have to take these to the Department of Health yourself," they said.

"Now?" I replied. It was a work-day.

"Any time," they said, "there's always someone there."

I went to the office and put the bag on a shelf

above my desk, where it hovered above me all day.

That night after work I delivered them to some building on the East Side.

When I got there a lone security guard was sitting in the lobby.

"HIV/AIDS test?" he asked.

"Yes," I said.

He proceeded to put on a pair of gloves that wouldn't have been out of place at a Ranger's game, lifted-up what looked like a fireplace shovel and then beckoned me to place the test tubes on the shovel.

After I did he placed them into a small refrigerator, and I was done.

A week later I got a letter from the Department of Health that stated I was HIV negative.

I had to read it twice.

Negative in this case was good.

I hadn't thought for a moment I was HIV positive, but prior to that week I hadn't thought about it all.

It was all I had thought about since I dropped off the blood though, and while I was relieved, I couldn't help but think about all of the people who were receiving different results.

That was when I started volunteering at Gay Men's Health Crisis.

—

Several months into the internship Bob was hired by the organization. He was a gay minister, balding and bearded, with round rosy cheeks and a big smile. He was also a licensed therapist and he asked me if I wanted to co-facilitate an HIV/AIDS support group with him. It would be for men and women, both gay and straight.

I jumped at the chance.

The group was comprised of Beth, a straight woman whose former husband had been exposed to HIV while on a business trip to the far east, and who she blamed for both her HIV status and her son's spina bifida; Jess, the group's Gandalf and unofficial leader, a bearded gay man who had lived longer with the virus than any other client at the agency; Brad, a married guy who had tried to live a straight life, but who, with his wife's blessing, had eventually turned to late night trysts with other men; and Carl, a handsome, angry, recovering substance abuser, who had been exposed to the virus while shooting Heroin and sharing needles with his fellow addicts.

The group met weekly for ninety minutes and always started with a check-in—how were things going that week, what was new, how was everyone feeling and so on. Everyone was asked to participate and then share a topic they wanted the group to discuss in greater depth. Such topics might include dating—for example, at what point did you share with someone that you were HIV positive and what was the best approach for dealing with the likely repercussions when you did. Another topic that received a lot of attention was drug combinations, and while protease inhibitors were still somewhat off on the horizon, the sheer amount of drug options available, how to take them, and the varying side effects were a constant source of tension and hope.

Check-in was always stressful for me.

I was expected to participate, but I felt uncomfortable focusing on exams, wedding planning and the other kinds of things I was dealing with.

My issues were not life-and-death matters, my fate was not so uncertain, and as a result, I remained detached, present for the group during the check-in, but not fully engaged.

One night I started to share some of my usual cursory commentary—"the fucking train took forever to get here tonight"—and Carl exploded.

"C'mon man," he screamed, "say something real, tell us something about your life that's fucking you up. You gotta get down in the muck with us, man."

I paused and looked around the room at the half-dozen pairs of eyes now staring at me and waiting for a response.

"All right, fine," I said, "I spent this past weekend in

New York City looking at wedding sites, and you know we're just not going to find anything, we have no idea what we want; we thought it would be nice to do something small, but now everyone is talking to us about all the people we need to invite; and we don't know whether we want flowers or not because they're so expensive, and then they just go and die, sorry you guys; do we prefer the photojournalist who refuses to take the group shots we're not even sure we want or the cookie-cutter professional wedding photographer who is willing to take them; do we think we need a videographer, a fucking videographer, are you kidding; and then there's the whole music thing, do you get a DJ or a band, and either way, do you play the fucking *Macarena* if people ask for it? And if all that isn't enough, we have to talk about this shit every night, and when we do my legs start to itch, and it's clearly stress, and it is driving me *fucking* crazy. So, how's that, better?"

Nobody spoke for a moment.

"That's what I'm talking about, man," Carl said with a big smile. "We want to know what healthy people struggle with. It takes our minds off things."

After that we were cool. I shared, I listened. I was part of things.

And it was good until the end of the year was upon us, my internship was over, and I had lingered into the summer as long as I could before I really needed to move onto the new school year and my new internship.

One night near the end of my time there, Carl got very animated during check-in.

"I have this asshole junkie friend," he said, "his name is Greg and he got exposed sharing a needle just like I did. Thing is, he won't tell his girlfriend. Too scared he says. He's a fucking jerk. He's not going to tell her? That's bullshit. Fuck that."

Greg.

Junkie.

Won't tell girlfriend.

I leaned forward in my seat, trying not to appear too interested.

"So, what did you do?" Bob asked. "Did you speak to him about this?"

"Did I speak to him?" Carl said. "Are you fucking kidding me? I fucking spoke to her, and I told her myself. Fuck him that selfish bastard."

Boom.

There it was, some finality and no better ending to the experience could have been written.

Well, but one, maybe.

I finish my second internship. I finish school. And I land a position on a Federal demonstration project working with homeless individuals with serious mental illness.

One of the programs at the organization I work for provides housing services to people with HIV/AIDS.

Since my work in the field things have changed dramatically, suddenly, protease inhibitors now exist, and are available, and people with access to them have mostly stopped dying.

It's not a cure, but the disease can be managed now, and if that's not the case for everyone, it has the potential to be soon.

One Sunday in *The New York Times Magazine* there is a piece on men and women with HIV/AIDS who have survived because of protease inhibitors, but didn't expect to, spent all of their money assuming there was no reason not to and now have to figure out how to live with no savings, when their plans were all about dying.

I ask the Director of the HIV/AIDS housing services program if he read the piece.

He is a handsome man with mottled skin, a gaunt face and cheekbones so sharp he must risk tearing his T-shirts when he pulls them on over his head.

"I'm that guy," he says. "I bought my dream condo, why not, right, and now I have to live in it, knowing that I'm not going to die, but have no money to survive on. I had no plans to live, why would I?"

He says this with a smile, rueful certainly, but a smile still.

He's alive, there is hope and he hadn't been counting on any of that.

At some point I'm asked attend a meeting with a number of substance abuse agencies so we can talk about the ways we can work together on behalf of our mutual clients.

One of the Executive Directors who has been planning to attend the meeting calls to say he can't come, but that he plans to send one of his supervisors instead.

When I walk into the meeting room I see Carl.

He's wearing a shirt and tie. He looks a little stiff, and his collar looks a little tight, but he also looks good, healthy, with color in his cheeks, no anger and a big smile on his face.

"How are you doing man?" I say, both happy and incredulous to see him.

"Never better," he says.

BE COOL

Here's the deal, Debbie is turning 30, and my idea is that we will go to Los Angeles, which in my mind remains the epitome of cool; sun-drenched and languid; overflowing with celebrities, movie sets, scandals, beaches, pool parties, and fake boobs; and so much alcohol and cocaine pouring down the streets that it's like the adult version of *Cloudy With A Chance of Meatballs*.

I suppose I could take a moment and consider the endless and soul-crushing moments being suffered in L.A. on a minute to minute basis as dreams are derailed and the reality that most everyone who chooses to live there is more likely to end-up sucking someone's dick for rent money in an alley than achieve even a modicum of the fame they seek.

But I don't have to think about any of that, I'm just hoping that we, me, can feel cool, or get a taste of it anyway, and why should I look at other's failures and despondency as a metaphor for what may come to pass on our trip?

I shouldn't, I won't, plus, it's so sunny there.

That said, what does it say about my own insecurities that I plan chunks of our trip to L.A. based on an article in the Travel section of *The New York Times* about what's cool in L.A. now, like right now, hence already passed?

It probably says a lot, but I choose to ignore that, because when said article promises that George Clooney hangs out at a certain bar, and the hippest, underground comedy will be happening at a club while we are there, I am content to look past my own inadequacies and focus on the bigger picture, my incessant need for star fucking in all its forms.

The first day we are in L.A. we go for drinks at the Polo Lounge, which is renowned for its awesome amounts of pinkness and unparalleled access to celebrities.

After we are seated I notice that Nastassja Kinski is sitting at the next table, deep in conversation.

I had Nastassja Kinski's pre-pubescent, naked, snake poster on my wall as a boy and I jerked-off to her image a lot. As I look at her I wonder if she knows this about me or at least assumes that any male my age probably has done the same.

I also try to get Debbie's attention, subtly of course, which to be frank, fails a little, when I realize Nastassja is glaring at me, something which is sort of cool when you think about it, but only sort of, especially when you factor in the resulting hard-on.

"Do you really believe that George Clooney just hangs out here," Debbie says on Day Two as we walk-up to a bar now long lost to history where George Clooney surely hangs out or once did.

"Yes," I say trying to sound confident, "he goes out just like we do, well, he's probably banging starlets at the end of the night, and he lives with a pig, and he probably doesn't stalk anyone, but other than that he's just like us, really."

The line to get into said bar is immense and roiling, packed with short skirts, cleavage and skinny legs.

The cover charge is surreal.

We pause.

We are not naifs, but as my underdeveloped plan un-furls I am no longer confident about where our journey is taking us. Sometimes during a pause, you find insight and inner peace, a path mysteriously emerging from your previous state of confusion and conflict.

Other times, you stand near a door just long enough

that a black, turtle-neck wearing George Clooney walks out of it moments later, George Clooney who is slighter than he appears on screen, yet somehow better looking, much better looking.

Our pause is now fortuitous, but what do we do next? Do we follow him as he leaves?

We don't have to, because he stops, right there in front of us, and just stands there, epic and beautiful, everyone in the area briefly frozen in place, all *Matrix*-like and slo-mo, the peace only shattered by the sudden appearance of a twitchy—pre-Ari Gold, still John Cusack's sidekick, one-time love interest of a friend at home who broke it off when he showed-up with a face smelling of woman— Jeremy Piven.

Piven is wrangling a group of women and clearly leveraging his proximity to Clooney to close the deal, which by all appearances he does as they disappear into the night.

There is no time for living off of one's previous successes in the City of Angels, however, and so on Day Three, I invite Eric, an old friend and long-time denizen of Los Angeles, to join us as we go out to the Luna Lounge for underground comedy.

I should say here, that then as now, anything considered underground possesses a certain cache of coolness for me. Seeing George Clooney certainly rocks, but even that is no comparison to potentially stumbling onto someone who no one knows, yet is potentially destined to be the next big thing.

I want this for Debbie, I really do, terribly even, but let's be honest, I really want it for me, and for all the moments down the road when we can say, "We were there when…"

Now, did I know it was black comic night at the Luna Lounge the day we chose to go? I did not.

Is there something inherently cool in not knowing this? Maybe, it depends on the pay-off. But when three Jews walk into such a club, and all the other Jews already there are hiding in the back behind their clunky black glasses and taking up all the tables, leaving us only the one table in front of the stage, and Eric, who knows what's to come, says, "Uh-oh, too late to leave now," should that serve as a red flag for someone, me, otherwise blinded by the City of Lights?

That depends on how you feel about every single joke for the next hour focusing on whites, Jews, and white Jews, if not in the actual set-up of the jokes, then the punch lines.

Which raises a question, is it in fact cool to roll with that onslaught one excruciating minute after the next?

Maybe, but is it somewhat unbearable? Definitely.

Until, just like our Clooney moment, there is a pause.

The comic in front of us is talking drugs, and then

looking right at us, he says, "Well everyone knows that white people use heroin, you've used heroin, right white people?"

He then pauses for dramatic effect. What will be funny apparently is our non-response, or better yet, our nervous demurrals. Who would admit to such a thing?

Not me, apparently.

However, Eric who has done many drugs, which I know after having done many drugs with him, responds in a completely nonplussed fashion.

"Of course we've done heroin," he says, "as you said, all white people have."

The comic leans back and scrunches up his face, flummoxed, and unsure how to continue. We sit there. He stands there. He never regroups and he is escorted from the stage.

No one mocks us after that, and soon enough, we triumphantly drive off into the sunset to Canters Deli for late night Egg Creams and revelry.

And it is only then, sitting there in this bastion of old Hollywood that I realize I have finally achieved a modicum of what I so clearly craved all along—a moment in the spotlight to call my own.

THE VAMPIRE DIARIES

I was a vampire and this was before they were cool, again, or sold books anyway.

I was out there at night, studying the *Reader* and *New City*, reading newsletters, lurking in the shadows, and trawling for victims, desperately in need of nourishment.

It wasn't blood that I craved however, it was words, and a voice of my own, not that I knew what that was, much less that such a phrase existed.

Further, it wasn't dark alleys or lonely bedrooms I haunted, but bookstores, the now long gone, but still missed Barbara's on Wells and Quimby's, and clubs like the Hideout and Metro.

Nor was it nubile virgins I stalked, but writers all the writers I could consume.

And I was insatiable.

It was mid-1990's Chicago and I was a carpetbagger, drawn here by the University of Chicago and the belief that its gothic halls and omnipresent Gargoyles would provide a change of scene—aesthetically and otherwise—from my incessantly dreggy, and yes, druggy, upstate New York undergraduate experience.

I needed to go to a great school, to wander its dusty halls and smell its erudite smells.

But it wasn't enough, because just as a vampire may substitute animal blood for human blood in a pinch, but not truly get what they need to survive, the University of Chicago, and more specifically, the social work school, which I loved, still wasn't what I wanted or needed.

I just didn't understand that yet.

Actually, that's not true, strike that, I understood it, I'm just telling you the narrative I carried in my head then, and possibly even one I think feels more dramatic, or cinematic, now.

Boy heads west to seek his fortunes and find himself, again, and what he finds is not what he expected to find, but something else, something that is grand, and transformative, and happened to be lying there dormant the whole time, just waiting to be discovered.

Which he does, because of Chicago and its broken nose, and the masses of words floating down the river, and alighted on the endless winds, jumbled, and tactile, and there, so right there, and just waiting to be plucked.

All of which is to say, that I knew what I wanted, and I had for years.

I wanted to be a writer, I just could not accept it, or taste it, or believe it was possible, much less grab it by the fucking neck and make it my own.

The problem, or if you prefer the positive reframe, and why not be positive, right, this is an origin story after all, is that I may not have been able to write, and I may have been a social worker, and no-account carpetbagger, ex-pat, slumming in the best little big town in the world, but there were writers everywhere, reading every night, all kinds, and they were just waiting for me, laying their trap and inviting my inevitable literary downfall.

Who were they? Who weren't they?

Elizabeth Crane. Joe Meno. Aleksander Hemon. Neil Pollack. Linda Barry. Scott Haim. Patrick McCabe. Junot Diaz. Dave Eggers. Cornel West. Dorothy Allison. Alex Kotlowitz. Sherman Alexie. John Irving. Saul Bellow. Spencer Dew. Gwendolyn Brooks. Art Spiegelman. Scott Turow. Studs Terkel. Jonathan Kozol. Henry Louis Gates, Jr. Bret Easton Ellis. Jim Carroll. Merrill Markoe. David Sedaris. Don DeGrazia.

And on and on and on.

All I had to do was throw a rock, and go wherever it landed, or even just leave the house, or whatever bar I was in and I was bound to stumble into a reading.

Which is what I did in an all-out effort to imbibe on their energy, steal their mojo, and make myself them, or at least something like them—a writer, because what could be better or more necessary than that?

Nothing.

I know I sound like a sociopath, or a stalker, but that's because I was, and I still am.

I prefer vampire, however, and not because it's sexier—though it is, and I'm hoping it will conjure up images of Robert Pattinson in your head as you think about me roaming the streets—but because vampires need to feed to survive, there's no other way, and I was desperately trying to survive, and Chicago, and its literary scene, embraced that and accepted me and all my needy, literary fuckedupedness.

It was magical.

Now could this have also happened when I lived in New York City before moving here, or San Francisco, before that?

It seems like that would have to be the case, how couldn't it have been?

I saw Ken Kesey do a reading in San Francisco when I first moved there, the only reading I somehow ever went to while I was living there, and I will never forget his response when someone asked him if he had a mission that guided his writing.

He started to sing:

"Sometimes the light's all shining on me, other times I can barely see, lately it occurs to me, what a long strange trip it's been."

But even having that memory seared into my brain, the fact is, if the literary scenes in those cities were ready for me, I wasn't ready for them.

Chicago though—the home of Mike Royko, Nelson Algren, Richard Wright and Gwendolyn Brooks—it was both ready for me, and I was ready for it.

And yet, if this is truly an origin story, there would have to be some kind of trigger, my crossroads moment, or something, right? Of course, and so how did it start, how did all of this stolen energy and insane need, translate to words on paper?

In my case it was a phone call, and not one even to me, but to my wife.

"She's leaving her husband," Debbie said, looking at me, shaken, "she's sitting in her car, bags packed, baby asleep and she's going to leave."

That was it.

Debbie went to sleep, fitfully, but she slept. I could not. I couldn't get the call out of my head, and I could not sleep.

There were too many voices, and too many ideas, and

after a lifetime of not be able to sleep, and doing all sorts of things to address it—staring at the ceiling, running, masturbating, watching television, reading, changing beds, and rooms, getting high, or drunk, and sometimes laid, anything to sleep, I did something I had never done before: I wrote a story.

The story was titled "Leaving Home," and I had written, and re-written, it many times in my head already. It was about someone who wants to leave their family. The protagonist wasn't a woman though like our caller had been, it was me, or some version of me, but it was sitting there, it had been for years, like a plane circling an airport and waiting for its turn to land.

I knew the structure, the rhythm and dialogue.

It was a download.

I had finally written something and I haven't stopped since.

Since then, I've had the opportunity to read at that Barbara's on Wells, which no longer exists, Quimby's, and the Hideout, and dozens of other places.

And I write.

So, is it because of Chicago?

Is there something magical about being here, or is that just magical thinking, born from the need to have a narrative, an origin story, and an explanation of why something that was so fucking hard for so long, and something I believed I could not live without, yet somehow could not do, is now something I actually do, just like that, or like this, that I'm doing now.

Maybe it is magical thinking, but is there anything wrong with that?

I don't know.

It's more interesting certainly than saying I just wasn't ready, that I didn't understand that I didn't truly need to consume other's words, because I had them waiting for me, and I just needed to start.

What I do know though, is that sometimes people ask me if I would be a writer if not for Chicago, and I say I just don't know, but I'm glad I didn't have to find out.

This is my home now, my children were born in Chicago I find myself living and dying with the Bears, I met all of the writers I first considered friends here, I work with Chicago publishers, and all of that is a narrative I gladly embrace.

Other people will ask: how does it feel to be a Chicago writer?

And to them I say, I'm not sure that I am a Chicago writer.

I don't say this because I don't want to be, I would be honored to be one, but only as long as it's okay with writers such as Joe Meno, Gina Frangello, Don DeGrazia, Billy Lombardo, Joseph Peterson and Michael Czyzniejewski, writers who can claim the city as their place of birth, and not merely as a place where they found themselves.

If it's okay with them, than its okay with me, because where else could I possibly find "a lovely so real?"

2000 – NOW

THE LONG HAUL

The smart thing of course would be to not run to-day at all. Last night I went to listen to Ike Reilly at Schubas and many beers were drunk.

I got home late and after watching television and gabbing with Debbie for an hour, I didn't sit down to write until 2:30 in the morning.

That got me to bed at 3:30 in the morning, and then back up at 7:30 to get the boys ready for school.

Then after that it was time for my annual physical, for which I have been fasting since midnight, clear liquids only—I am allowed to drink coffee, but have not.

At the physical I give blood and have a prostate exam.

I walk to the supermarket from the doctor's office, so I can help Debbie carry the groceries back to the house.

We get home and watch the latest winner of American

Idol perform on Oprah.

I am hungry, I am tired and I am sluggish.

It is now almost noon, and I still haven't had any coffee.

I held off on eating so I could run, which I expected to do much sooner, and the smart thing of course would be to not run today at all.

And yet, I can eat later, I can sleep later, I can drink coffee later, but there's no guarantee that I will be able to run later.

Shit happens.

I'm gone.

There is a long run I do that has been my standby for the fifteen years we have lived in this neighborhood; but between work and family and a brutal winter, I haven't hit this one as regularly as I normally once did.

I'm going to hit it today, though.

I head up Dearborn and into Lincoln Park—past the famous Saint-Gaudens statue of Lincoln himself—and down through the underpass where the homeless reside during the winter and the spiders spin their big-ass webs all summer.

I am excited about this route after having had a break from it, but it's a tricky run for me in many ways; or, well, maybe just one way.

After all, it's not a hard run and there are no hills or

weird terrain.

There's almost no traffic and, as a whole, the running paths are wide and free of bikers and dogs.

No, the problem is psychological.

During our early years here in Chicago, this run took me about 52 minutes on a good day and on more recent years it's been closer to an hour; but due to a combination of an arthritic knee and sleep problems with the boys during the winter a year ago, I ended up going through one of the worst stretches of running I've ever experienced.

Eventually things got better—the boys' sleep problems seemed to fade, the arthritis receded for a moment—and one night when I went on the run I decided to time myself.

67 minutes.

Fuck.

I knew I had been running slower, but I wasn't ready to actually be slow; or worse, accept that I'm getting older and that some of this is inevitable.

I also didn't think I had to go down without a fight.

Did I?

I am now passing the Latin School soccer field and wrapping onto the foot path.

I run along the lagoon where the scullers row morning and night and where the geese stop over during their annual migration to wherever it is that they go.

This run has four evenly divided sections to it; and so after recording my sad old-man 67-minute run, I decided to start trying to get as close to fifteen minutes for each section as I could. It still wouldn't get me to 52 minutes, but it would at least be closer to an hour, and that I've decided I can live with.

67 minutes quickly became 62, and then grudgingly became 59, then 58, and on a good day 57.

One morning during the fall I hit 55 minutes.

It was completely triumphant and completely crushing all at once; because although I was happy with the time, I didn't feel good—not when I finished, not after I showered, nor all day at work.

My back was sore.

I felt queasy.

And there was some unfortunate and poorly situated chafing that just doesn't happen at slower speeds.

Worse, though, was the thought that while I simply might not ever be able to replicate 52 minutes again, now that I had run the route in 55 minutes, I would have to obsessively try, because any time I did the route I would wonder if I wasn't trying hard enough—adding a psychological blow to whatever weakened state would result from my attempts to achieve whatever had transpired that one morning in the first place.

—

I head under the second overpass of the run and pass the unofficial fifteen-minute mark, though I have decided against looking at my split times for each of the sections because I don't want to get depressed.

I am pain-free, which is always nice; but I am not spry, although I don't know if this means anything for how the run will end.

I never feel wholly good during the first quarter of any run, at any distance; I am still not loose and my head is still not completely in it.

Another thing affecting me today is not just this invisible bar I've set for this particular route that now haunts my every step, but that I never even try anymore to run fast on any other route but this one and so I haven't attempted to run fast at all for months.

Further, it's light out, and all sunny and warm, none of which is conducive for speed; not for me anyway.

I pass the driving range and head in closer to the lake, approaching the totem pole at Addison and the halfway point of the route.

There are a lot of runners out today.

I can see them out of the corner of my eye, and I can feel one of them coming up on me.

I would like to tell you that I don't mind being passed, that this is not a competition for me, but I would be lying.

When this guy finally passes me, I pick it up a notch.

It does not feel good.

Not bad, necessarily, just not good.

There's no electricity, no juju; and while I may not be bonking, I just don't have much in the tank today either.

I start to obsess over the fact that I must be tired, that I'm not hydrated or caffeinated, that I have given blood and that I'm not even quite halfway done.

Motherfucker.

Luckily, I am juggling multiple obsessions today; I have also been talking to a literary agent for the first time.

It is terrifying, though not because of any particular fear of being rejected, which is always a bummer, but is also an incessant part of being an artist, and thus best to simply ignore.

No, I am more freaked out by the fact that she may want to work with me. Or, strike that; she has been working with me, but I'm freaked out by the fact that it might be successful.

What then?

I don't think I overly pride myself on being an outsider, loved by just a few readers here and there; having nurtured my writing outside the world of MFAs, workshops and conferences, this is simply how it's worked out for me, and is the path I've chosen to take.

Okay, maybe that's somewhat disingenuous, and maybe I do enjoy whatever "outsider" status it is I think I possess, but I don't think it's been holding me back or making me less ambitious, has it?

I always thought the whole effort was about improving my craft and seeking opportunities, and that like with running, when my skill level and the right opportunity converged I would grab it.

Which is what this agent represents, an opportunity that I am thrilled by, have grabbed onto and don't plan to let go of.

I make the turn for the second half of the run and start working my way back home.

I know I've picked up the pace, but I can't tell how much.

I still feel terrible, and in the daylight I can never quite get my bearings anyway.

I try not to obsess over blood and food.

I sent the agent a mostly final draft of what I like to believe could be my third novel.   It's the story of a guy who is married and trying not to sleep with his intern. He's also scared to have a baby and would prefer not to kill his neighbor. More than that, however, he's smart enough to know that he should be more curious about his life and his decisions, that he shouldn't be so reflexive in his decision-making, but he can't quite get there, instead losing himself in his confusion and his failure to communicate what this means to him and those around him, until things get shaken up with the birth of his child and the child's subsequent medical struggles.

I pass the three-quarter mark of the run and I have a decision to make—this part of the route, which directly follows the lakefront from Fullerton to the North Beach footbridge, is where fast runs go to die. I either hit this part with everything I have left, going for broke and trying to come in under an hour, or I let myself start to fade before I even reach the final stretch onto Dearborn and home.

I decide to go for it, pumping my arms and pushing forward.

My legs immediately feel sluggish and my breathing turns erratic.

Spittle starts to fly from my mouth and my nose begins to run over my lips and onto my collar.

My chest starts to throb and some weird cramp begins to crawl from my right shoulder into my neck.

I am actually seeing stars and begin to wonder if I am going to pass out.

Why didn't I eat?

Why did I go out at all?

Why am I pushing myself like this?

My form starts to break down, my arms jerky and my legs stiff.

This is a bad place for me; this is where my knee is most at risk of becoming inflamed.

By the time I reach the footbridge, I am having trouble breathing.

The agent thinks my dialogue is authentic and my characters are real. She seems excited about the book. But she wants to talk plotting.

Is the story too predictable? Are there subplots lacking closure?

Maybe.

Maybe I can do more with the hot opera-singing neighbor and her rock-star ass.

Maybe I can show more interaction between the various couples in the book as the story evolves.

And maybe the pregnancy itself can be explored in more depth.

Maybe there are a million things I can do if I think she's right and trustworthy and I am willing to take the plunge, seize whatever opportunity ultimately emerges, and push myself farther than maybe I am comfortable with.

Maybe.

—

I pull up in front of our apartment building and look at my time.

56 minutes.

Fuck yeah.

YOU WANT SOME CHEW?

I do not have a drinking problem.
   Though, my drink of choice is a Gin & Tonic and the fact that I have a drink of choice may in fact be a red flag.

   I do not have a drinking problem.

   Though, I have been drinking steadily, at times excessively, now for twenty-five years.

   I do not have a drinking problem, though even as I write this I am drinking a Bloody Mary, at home, at 2:00 p.m. in the afternoon as my son naps in the back.

   I do not have a drinking problem.

1983

This is not the first time I binge drink. That was one week

before at a graduation party. That night was full of joy. Laughter. Older girls. And triumph.

Despite all of that, I don't plan to drink that much again.

That kind of thinking will come later.

Here I am though, at another graduation party, it's late and I've drank a lot.

Billy walks over.

Billy is older than I am. He is very cool and very tough.

He is Tim Riggins sans the model good looks.

"You want some chew?" Billy says.

I don't say no to Billy.

"Sure Billy," I say, leaning on a tree for support.

I take the chew, jam it between my lip and gums as the Skoal commercials direct me to do, sit down at the base of the tree and promptly pass out.

When I awake I swallow the chewing tobacco in its entirety. This is followed by my violently throwing up everything I've ever eaten in my entire life.

As I lie there, Stacie comes over to check on me and wipe my brow.

Stacie is a sophomore and a star on the softball team.

Stacie is a babe.

I love Stacie.

This is not how I wanted to meet her.

After I recover, Stacie wanders off into the night and I end-up eating micro-waved macaroni and cheese on someone's cracked linoleum kitchen floor.

In hindsight, this probably could have been viewed as a lesson of some kind.

1984

Lara is rich and smart, a tennis player, and easily the most beautiful woman I have met during my first fifteen years on the planet.

She is the Tyra to my Landry and unavailable to me for all the obvious reasons.

If her sheer unatainability isn't bad enough though, I also have a deal with my friend Arnie that we will never, ever, date each other's former paramours and so even if something freakish were to happen, like say Lara briefly losing her mind, she would still fall onto this list of untouchables.

And so it is until tonight's party.

Because on this evening, and after many, many Genesee Cream ales, Lara apparently does lose her mind and I apparently decide that I don't care all that much about lifelong friendships.

While this is probably another sign of some kind, I allow Lara to lead me to a bedroom where she proceeds to lie down on top of everyone's winter coats look up at me and smile.

I should add here, that at this point I have never been to second base, and so as I survey the situation, it is all I can think about.

Being the early 1980's however, and winter in upstate New York, there are some challenges:

I must remove her L.L. Bean rag wool sweater.

Her father's Brooks Brother's pinstripe oxford.

A tight fitting Ralph Lauren, pique polo shirt.

A white, tighter still Izod turtleneck.

A T-shirt that reads "All This and Brains Too."

And then a dreaded, front snap bra which requires me to do a semi, one-handed push-up after a dozen beers while on top of dozens of shifting corduroy CB ski jackets.

Still, like Roger Bannister, Edmund Hillary and Tenzing Norgay before me, and despite breaking a vow to a one-time best friend, I accomplish what can only be described as an epic feat, albeit only epic to me, as it has been done before, and will have no great, or lasting, impact on the world—well, outside of my personal version of it anyway—whatsoever.

1986

Jennifer has made it clear to me that she does not sleep

with friends and does not intend to do so tonight even if it is the prom. She says this with her legs wrapped around my waist and her prom grown somewhere up above her own as we sit in the den of my friend Jake's house, whose parents have given us their home, stocked the bar and are staying in a hotel for the night, something that was very 1980's and most certainly illegal now.

Jennifer was my first kiss in Eighth grade.

We also made out drunkenly on someone's lawn in Tenth grade.

But I've made no assumptions that we would have sex, and I am sleeping with someone else who I should have clearly brought to the prom anyway, and so when Jennifer preemptively says no to sex I wasn't counting on, I say fine, and proceed to drink with Jake and Larry—two other guys who aren't getting any—at the bar.

After we proceed to polish off a two liter bottle of Absolut Vodka in the length of time it takes us to watch an episode of SportsCenter, Jennifer magically appears.

"Dude," she says, "I've changed my mind."

Nice.

There are no rooms left though, and so we hit the kitchen floor.

Maybe it's the alcohol, or the fact that I'm now thinking about how much I might really want to be with that other person, but despite Jennifer's most valiant efforts, I cannot complete the transaction for the first time in my still very nascent sexual life.

This maybe should have been a lesson learned as well, something like alcohol giveth, and alcohol taketh away, but if so, I will fail to learn this lesson as well, and repeatedly at that.

We go to sleep and later that week Jake's father tells me how he came home that next morning because he forgot to bring a tie with him, but after seeing Jennifer and I lying naked on the kitchen floor he decided he was too scared to proceed any farther into the house.

1987

I am madly in love with my friend Debbie though she has zero interest in me. She's got long skinny legs and long brown hair. We go to college together at SUNY Albany, watch *Days of Our Lives*, drink at O'Heaney's and eat Slim Jims.

Tonight we are at Ralph's and we are at Ralph's because they do not proof, on Fridays you can buy half-pitchers of Long Island Ice Tea for three dollars each, and oh yes, she is supposed to be meeting some other guy there.

After an hour, Debbie has had three half-pitchers and I have had five.

She goes to talk to the guy and I pretend to be the

dutiful and supportive friend who is not remotely, much less, insanely jealous.

She returns and asks me to walk her to the bathroom.

She pushes on the door to no avail.

She leans her back against the door to catch her breath.

She is beautiful.

I am staring at her, and I do not care, it's all I want to do.

She suddenly grabs me by the neck and kisses me hard on the lips.

It is the greatest first kiss ever recorded.

Poets will write about it.

It will be taught in classes.

It will cement a relationship we didn't even know we had yet.

By all rights it should never end, but sadly, we are interrupted.

"What the fuck, can I use the bathroom?" a girl with bad nose job says.

"It's locked," Debbie says.

"Yeah," she says, "do you mind if I try it?"

The girl pulls instead of pushes. The door opens. She rolls hers eyes, walks in and we are now too flummoxed and self-conscious to continue.

We go back to the dorm to watch *Miami Vice*— Crockett is marrying Sheena Easton—but after some more drinks we decide to make out in our friend Avi's bed instead.

It is all very nice until we sober up and actually have to talk about our feelings, a scenario that will play itself out again and again until we get it right.

1992

I should begin here by stating, that it's not as if like I don't drink between 1987 and 1992, truthfully, I was blacked out for lengthy stretches of this time period, but my primary focus during this time became consuming as many hallucinogens as I could, and so I will hold off on discussing this era in more depth until I write a piece on gateway drugs and beyond.

That said, in 1992 I go to see a therapist for the first, but certainly not the last time.

The therapist asks me if I think I have a drinking problem.

I say I do not.

"Ben, have you ever blacked out from drinking?" she asks.

"Of course," I say, "many times."

"That's a problem," she says.

"How?" I say truly incredulous. "Everyone passes out from drinking."

"No," she says, "they don't."

I have never heard this before, much less ever considered it a possibility.

"Really," I say, "because everyone I know has passed out from drinking."

"Has it ever occurred to you," she says, "that you may gravitate towards people with drinking problems?"

It had not until then, and I don't answer her, but just like Bruce Willis's character at the end of *The Sixth Sense* I start to replay my drinking over the years and who I drank with.

I realize now that I have always steered away from those who don't drink. I've never even really met those people, though I remember some of them now, and they seem like they may have been nice and fun to hang out with.

It is honestly one of the most profound moments I have ever experienced, and so armed with this new insight I do the smart thing, I stop seeing her.

1996

It is my Chicago bachelor party and we are at the old Ranalli's on Dearborn spending time with the lovely and talented Melanie Melons.

We are drinking, of course, and after Melanie leaves,

we decide to move the party to the original Iggy's.

On the way out, I slip a bottle of tequila into my pocket.

We drink at the bar for hours as we discuss the merits and drawbacks of getting married. It goes something like this:

"I'm sorry, why would you do this?" Bill says.

"Yeah, I don't know," I say.

"Good enough," Bill says.

We retire to the pool table on the outside deck and I remember the bottle of tequila.

I slip it out of my pocket and as I raise it to my lips I feel a hand come down on my shoulder.

I am dragged off of the deck, down the stairs, out the door, across the street and thrown against a chain-link fence.

The dude doing the dragging and throwing is enormous.

He is bald and wearing a black suit, the Ving Rhames guy.

His face is contorted into a ferocious mask of hate and rage.

He is fucking furious and looks like he may in fact explode.

"You bring alcohol into my house," he spits in utter disdain. "My house! You disrespect me like that? My dad would have beat my ass for such a transgression."

I remain calm.

I weather the outrage.

But it has never been more clear to me that even occasionally drinking alcohol the way I once did is becoming less and less manageable.

From this point on I drink less and less.

2000

I am in Atlanta for work and meet up with Vicky, an old friend I once drank with.

At dinner she consumes one drink after another as she reminisces about all the partying we did in college. She seems thrilled and nostalgic just thinking about it, but watching her I feel kind of sad and I hope I never sound like this anymore.

"Do you ever think we drank too much in college?" I finally ask. "I've begun to wonder whether or not we all had drinking problems back then."

It may be that I sound more self-righteous than I intend to, or it may be that I am acting all self-actualized when I'm really not, but I've never asked anyone this question before and it seems like a good time to start.

Vicky isn't having it.

"What the fuck are you talking about?" she says polishing off her drink and reaching for another. "No, no fucking way. It was totally normal behavior."

In retrospect, this may have been the wrong time, and wrong person to discuss this with, but she does remind me of someone I once knew and hope to never see again.

2001

There is a new therapist that things will go terribly awry with. I will feel bullied by him and he will feel that I have tried to manipulate him regarding his fees.

But before all of that—or maybe, probably, during it—there are nuggets of wisdom that he shares and that I embrace as truth.

"Ben do you think you have a drinking problem?" he asks me one day.

"Well, if the answer to that has something to do with blacking out, then no, I don't think so, I haven't blacked-out in years, and frankly, while I still sometimes drink too much, I now try not to exceed two drinks when I don't have to," I reply.

"Why do you think this is?" he asks me.

"I don't know," I say, "I guess I didn't feel like I could manage it anymore."

"No, that's not it," he replies. "It wasn't working for you anymore and as soon as you realized that, you made a change."

And he's right.

I may have no idea how to truly manage my compulsions, in fact I may just swap one compulsion for another—reading begets masturbation begets running begets alcohol begets drugs begets writing, rinse repeat—but the fact is, I need to write now, every day, I mostly only have time to do so at night, or so I believe, and when I drink I can't write, not like I want to, and that's just not going to work for me anymore.

2008

I make myself a Bloody Mary.

I sit down at the kitchen table.

And I start to write.

I have only one drink.

JESUS WALKS

Jesus came to me at work one day. Maybe that's not entirely accurate. I saw Jesus at work one day. No, that's not it either.

To see someone implies that they were there in flesh and blood, and that isn't what happened at all. Jesus did not walk into my office to get a check request signed or talk to me about seeing Criss Angel the night before at the House of Blues.

On the other hand, it wasn't a hallucination either.

Jesus was not some disembodied presence like you might see in the *Ghost and Mrs. Muir*.

Nor was seeing Jesus a feeling per se, like when someone tells you they've "found religion," or "I awoke to find Jesus inside of me," as my old girlfriend Sara once claimed when I found her at home with my old roommate Jesus kind of inside her.

Maybe I should just tell you what happened.

I was at my desk working on some very important correspondence. In fact, I was responding to an e-mail I had received from a Mister Isaiah, an attaché to the wife of the recently deposed Nigeria Finance Minister. She now lived in Switzerland and had limited cash on hand, but with my support, and a mere ten thousand unmarked American dollars, she could readily access the vast funds her husband had secreted away in the waning days of his job.

We were discussing how said exchanges take place, when I happened to look out the window at the Hotel Intercontinental which was across the street from my office.

The front of the hotel is a clear, curved bank of windows and as I looked at the windows most directly facing mine, I saw an image emerge out of the reflection of my very own building. There was a man in a long beige robe, his arms outstretched in prayer or welcome. There was a cross on his chest and behind him was a larger cross, also beige, and distinct enough to reflect that he was lying across it in what might have been repose, but could also very well have been crucifixion.

There was no face.

Instead there was a long almost horse-like visage, possibly a mask, protruding from the body. The image was clearly stone, the stone utilized to construct my building, and there was no sign of breath or movement, outside of the rare undulation caused by the shifting clouds, large trucks passing beneath or what I surmised might be the occasional expulsion of collective hotel gas.

I assumed Stone Jesus would go away, but he didn't, though that might be because neither my building nor the hotel itself had gone away. Still, while I knew in my heart that the vision was merely a reflection, I also believed it would move on if I ignored it, focusing instead on the totals of that week's *America's Got Talent* vote or *US Weekly's* current analysis of Betty White's alleged baby bump.

Stone Jesus did not budge though, instead choosing to float there, watching and waiting, not judgmental in any way, but not communicating either, happy seemingly to just get his God on, while floating majestically above the masses.

I knew Stone Jesus couldn't just be there for my benefit, but his appearance hadn't drawn any true believers seeking guidance either.

Nor had there been any miracles from what I could see, though it should be noted that after spotting Stone Jesus, the brunette summer intern had smiled at me, something I had prayed for any number of times late at night in the safety of my bed.

Wanting to know if others saw what I did I went to

visit Matt who occupies the office next to mine. I should say here that Matt is a sinner. He lies. He steals. And he has lain down with men.

Or so I've heard.

As far as Stone Jesus went though, Matt wasn't feeling it.

"I don't see anything dude," Matt said.

"You don't see that reflection there," I said, "Jesus in a robe, and those crosses, both the one on his chest and the one behind him, c'mon, really?"

"I guess I kind of see a cross," Matt said. "Are you okay buddy?"

"Okay? Of course," I said. "I'm great, never better. Why do you ask?"

"Just checking," Matt said.

"It's not like this is a John Denver thing," I said. "Though I do hope he's at peace now."

"Sure," Matt said, "whatever you say brother."

"Thanks," I said. "Now for the sake of argument, you are a sinner, right?"

"If you say so," Matt said.

"It's not me that says so," I said, "but we both know that you are going to burn in hell, and so maybe that has something to do with your obstinacy around seeing Stone Jesus? I mean that's a possibility, yes?"

"Maybe, sure," Matt said. "Now could you please take

your hands off of my neck, that kind of hurts?"

"Yeah, okay, fine," I said, "thanks anyway, and God speed."

I went back to my office. Stone Jesus was still looking at me and he still wasn't speaking, so I tried to read his body language.

Nothing, it was very frustrating.

I paused for a moment.

Stone Jesus was clearly there for a reason.

He had some larger purpose for me, a message, I knew it. I just didn't know what it was.

I decided to ask him myself.

"Stone Jesus, why have you come to me," I said, "and what are you trying to tell me?"

He didn't say. He just kept staring.

"Is it addressing world peace, or maybe global warming," I said.

Nothing, Stone Jesus was holding out on me.

"Dude," I said, "is it land mines or determining once and for all what happened in the last scene of *Sopranos*?"

No reply, maybe I was supposed to decide on my own?

That would be tough. I decided to pray on it, which was also tough. Should I kneel? Was I supposed to say something? And if so, was I supposed to say it out loud?

I decided I would just focus on staring out the window.

I stared really hard.

I stared until my eyes hurt, but nothing much was happening, not until I realized that Jesus, the stone version and otherwise, doesn't tell people what to do, that's so not his style.

There are signs you need to look for and interpret, like having to kill your firstborn son or being swallowed whole by a whale, and if you read these signs correctly it all begins to make sense.

I stopped praying then and began to look for signs, subtle things like swarms of locusts or burning bushes, shit like that.

Though I was just getting to know Stone Jesus, I knew he was not looking to draw attention to himself or make a scene, he is a simple guy and so the sign would be simple as well.

I just had to find it.

I looked some more. I tried to connect the dots, slowing things down as I sought out patterns and connections in the whir of activity on the sidewalk outside my building.

But there was nothing, nothing at all.

Why was this?

Stone Jesus was clearly real.

Why did none of this make sense?

Maybe it's because I do not believe in God, but there are times I wish I did?

Or maybe it's because I do not embrace religion, but when my dad became sick, and in the days after he died, I was jealous of those who found comfort in its traditions and strictures.

What did I have?

I had running, and writing, and a loving family, and I would eventually have therapy too, and that's a lot, but it wasn't always enough.

Not enough to make sense of the confusion certainly.

And then suddenly I had Stone Jesus.

He had come out of nowhere, but how couldn't he?

My parents did not merely keep religion at arm's length, they found it unnecessary.

Being Jewish, though, is complicated. You can renounce religion, but still feel strongly about Jewish culture.

I don't think my parents cared all that much if we knew anything about the Jewish holidays—there were only occasional stabs at Seders and visits to the local reformed temple—though we always celebrated Hannukah.

My father built towering menorahs out of the spare wood lying around his art studio. My brother Adam and I decorated them in all sorts of outlandish ways—adding feathers, and drawings, and the random detritus we stumbled onto throughout the house.

The photos from those years are consummate 1970's shots, and in them my brother and I are clamoring around that year's menorah like wild animals in tight velour shirts; my dad with his crazy hair and bushy mustache is unsmiling usually, holding one of us in place, his hand firmly on a shoulder; and my mom, is young and lovely, her long black hair pulled into two braids draped over the front of her shoulders.

We had thirteenth birthday parties, though not necessarily Bar Mitzvahs. Mine was in a basement pub located downtown. There was a pinball machine in the back. I insisted the cake be decorated with marzipan. There were no girls at the party. I was too embarrassed to invite any.

Adam's party was at the Holiday Inn Arena where we went for Mother's Day Brunch. It was held in the banquet room overlooking the river where the BC Pops did their July 4th summer concert on boats underneath the Court Street Bridge.

Adam, who was more studious than I, insisted on learning his Haftorah. He read it aloud from a dais provided by the hotel, the Holiday Inn logo displayed proudly for all to see.

My parents were also activists.

One time they argued about which of them was more dedicated to activism. My dad reminded my mom that he had scaled the White House fence during the Vietnam War. She reminded him that she was pregnant with me at the time.

We went to 25th Anniversary of the March on Washington. Adam and I ran through the crowds, racing to see how many people we could beat to the end.

During the summer of the bicentennial we marched in Philadelphia to support aid to cities on a day that was so hot even my parents wondered why we were there.

My parents felt most strongly about Israel though—a place they had both lived—and Israel's treatment of the Palestinians.

They traveled to Israel repeatedly over the years, visiting refugee camps, meeting with groups like Peace Now, and demonstrating with the Women in Black. They wrote about these trips in the local paper and spoke about them to all who would listen.

The Jewish community in the small town where we lived called my parents self-hating Jews, questioning Israeli policy being tantamount to questioning one's very existence, but they insisted this wasn't true—they were proud Jews and they loved Israel, they just couldn't condone these kinds of politics.

But these are just snapshots, scenes from a life, or lives, yet to be completed or fulfilled. There was a larger struggle there and it was about identity, choices and obligations.

My parents may very well have been conflicted about religion and culture, and undecided about what they felt

Adam and I should be exposed to, but it was my father who was truly in conflict, with his upbringing, with his life and with himself.

He wanted to immerse himself in art, but knew he had to take care of his children.

He wanted to be part of some larger community, yet reveled in his outsider status.

He wanted to reject religion, but remained torn because of his roots and his connection to Jewish culture.

My mother had grown-up in a home where religion was rejected outright. Her parents were Jewish, New York intellectuals. They were community organizers and social activists. They wanted nothing to do with organized religion.

My dad's childhood was different.

His family celebrated the Jewish holidays and he had grown up above a synagogue in the Bronx. As a child, he watched the members of the congregation come and go from his living room window. He was in awe of them— their singular focus, their sense of community—they had somewhere they fit in. He had never felt this way.

He had also been a Bar Mitzvah. We have the photos. They're black and white. My dad is in a dark suit. He is wearing a white tie. He looks so proud. He has accomplished something that is wonderful and valued.

On this day he can forget about his struggles in school;

the difficulties he has connecting with his father; and the improbability that a poor, Jewish kid will someday become an artist.

On this day he is a man and no one can take that away from him.

Later, as a teenager, my father lived on a kibbutz in Israel, as did my mom. At one point they even talked about moving there. Back then my dad was trying to run away from his family, the claustrophobic confines of his neighborhood and the oppressive mores of the 1950s.

He was trying to find a place he could call home.

He did these things, but in rejecting his family and his neighborhood, he rejected religion as well.

At one time maybe he had been at peace with this decision, but then everything changed. My father was diagnosed with a rare form of bone cancer and told that without treatment he might live another year and a half. He tried everything. Nothing worked. Not enough any way. He lived for another 16 months.

I saw him as often as I could.

While we had always talked about any number of things from shooting pool to the latest Jim Jarmusch movie, we now began to talk about religion as well, and Judaism in particular, things we had rarely ever touched on.

He looked back over his life and he questioned whether he had made the right choices. Was he sick because he had not been more religious or because he had not moved to Israel?

He just did not know.

And I had no answers for him, I didn't know enough to say.

When my father first became ill he befriended a Chasidic Rebbe. My grandmother had given my dad a book written in Hebrew. It had text from the Kabbalah and it was supposed to help keep evil away. My father reached out to the Rebbe hoping he could help him translate the text. After this, they began to talk and as they did my father began to revisit Judaism and all that he'd left behind.

During the last months of his life my father was hospitalized and the Rebbe offered to perform a Yom Kippur service in his room. My father readily agreed.

The room was white, sterile, and cold, spotless, but for the sections of *The New York Times* strewn about the chairs and floor.

The Rebbe was decked out in a somewhat scruffy black overcoat and suit, he had a fedora pulled down tightly around his head, and his paes' were like untended vines, crazy, free to roam, and curling into his fantastically full reddish brown beard.

He came to my father's room with his young daughters and a student who was there to blow the shofur.

As the Rebbe began the service, my dad began to cry.

Soon the little girls joined their father and began to sing.

My dad cried some more.

Near the end of the ceremony, the young student blew the shofur.

Seven times he blew the shofur and each time he did my father cried even harder.

The student then finished and the ceremony was over.

The Rebbe wished us well and they left.

And then there we were, my father, mother, and I, drained, alone, and back in the hospital room they had briefly transported us from.

My mother asked my father what he had been feeling as he cried.

He said that with each note of the shofur he felt he was being healed.

My father has been dead for fifteen years.

I miss him and I miss what might have been.

My world has since opened anew.

I am now a father myself.

I still do not believe in God, but I do wonder what kind of god would strike down a man before his time?

And is it that the same god who can give me a gift as precious as that of my children?

It might be that if I had more faith in something, any-thing, I would know the answers to these questions.

But I don't, and I just can't make sense of any of it.

My father never quite found peace and I don't want to repeat that.

Nor do I want to pass this legacy on to my children.

And so here I am, I still do not know if I care about religion, but I do contemplate its importance. I also do not know what I think my children's relationship with religion should be, but I do ponder what role I am supposed to play in exposing them to Jewish culture and its traditions.

Part of the struggle of course is not knowing what my sons need now or will need as adults, and part of the struggle is recognizing that even with death and birth, nei-ther religion, God or anything remotely spiritual has ever truly spoken to me.

Stone Jesus came to me though at a moment when I needed something.

It gave me something to focus on, brought me hu-mor and even briefly transported me away from a troubled, confusing time in my life.

All of which I greatly appreciate, but here I am again, and where is that, nowhere, and while nothing nearly as tragic as my father's death is in the air, the boys are grow-ing-up, and I find myself wondering if writing, running, love and humor will be enough the next time things are tough and I'm not sure, where I, or they, will be able to seek solace.

MY (NOT QUITE) CANCER YEARS

My Wife Stabs Me in the Back While I Sleep.

I awake in a cold sweat writhing in pain. My wife has stabbed me in the lower back. I cannot stand or walk. It hurts to breath. It hurts not to breathe. I go see our general practitioner Dr. W. Dr. W. is short and dark. He has a bunch of kids. He looks to be about 15 years old. He likes to talk about dieting.

(1999)

My Wife Did Not Actually Stab Me in The Back.

I have not actually been stabbed in the back. My wife would not do that. Not in my sleep anyway. She would stab me in the stomach so her face was the last thing I saw. Dr.

W. isn't sure what's going on. Then again, he never is. Is it a kidney stone? I ask. No, he says. Remember that Seinfeld where Kramer has a kidney stone? he asks. Sure. Remember how he was walking? Yes. You would look more like that. So, what it is then? I think it could be a virus interacting with your kidneys, he says. Really? Yeah, let's run some blood tests and check your urine. Ok. Ok. The pain subsides. It is not a virus. But there are some malformed cells floating around in my urine.

(1999)

Herman Munster Tells Me He is Going to Put a Camera in My Penis.

Dr. W. sends me to see Dr. F. Dr. F. is an Urologist. He has a square jaw and a head like Herman Munster. His neck is always red and irritated. He doesn't say much. So, what do you think? I ask. I think it's probably a kidney stone, he says. Really? Yes, he says, or a tumor. A tumor? Yes, but that's doubtful at your age. So, what do we do, I ask. A Cystoscopy, he says. What's that? We're going to look inside your bladder and see what's there. And how do you do that? I ask. There's a tube and a camera and we go through your penis. Yeah, so, I'll be asleep for that, right? No. No? No, you'll be awake and we'll do it right here in the office, he says.

(1999)

Herman Munster Puts My Dick in a Clamp.

I return one-week later. The room is cold, and bare, just a table and a monitor. Dr. F asks me to strip from the waist down and cover myself with the sheet. He leaves. I strip. I lie there. I wait. And wait some more. I read the sports page. Dr. F. returns. He pulls out a clamp. And what's that for? I ask. It holds the penis in place during the procedure, he says. Dr. F. pulls the sheet down and adjusts the clamp. He then pulls out a plastic tube, maybe half an inch across, and a couple feet in length. This is the scope, he says, we need to insert this. How, I say, I mean really? He does not respond. He takes out a tube of some unidentified lubricant. He coats the scope and then inserts it into my penis. There is a pinch and then there is movement. It burns a bit. It's also kind of titillating. Dr. F manipulates the tube until it reaches my bladder, and then moves it around. He is searching for something, anything. We track his progress on the monitor. He doesn't find a thing. No tumor, no stone, not even a trail of residue the stone might have left behind. You probably passed the stone between visits, he says. Wouldn't I have felt that? I ask. Not necessarily, he says. What can I do to prevent this from happening again? I say. We don't really know, he says, drink lots of water, avoid too much ice tea. That's it? I ask. Well, that and get on with your life, he says.

(1999)

I Get On With My Life Until Everything Feels Fucked.

I get on with my life. Until the blood that is. It's not like I haven't had blood in my urine before. But back then I was playing ultimate Frisbee and running marathons. And back then my father hadn't died from a rare form of Cancer. Dr. W. isn't so sure he knows what's going on. I'm going to send you back to Dr. F., he says. Oh, and by the way, he adds, I've lost 15 pounds on my new diet. Yeah? Yeah, no carbs, no sugar and a Diet Coke when I want some pop. Think about it.

(2001)

Harmless Malformations.

Dr. F. is happy to see me. I think, maybe, who knows. You could have a stone trapped in your bladder that is rubbing on the bladder's lining, he says. Really? Yes, and that could be causing the bleeding, he continues. He orders an IVP. This is a test where you drink some dye and it allows them to X-ray your internal organs. I get an IVP. The results are murky and there is a dark spot. It could just be a spot on the X-ray, Dr. F. says, or it could be something else. Like what, a stone? I say. Yes, he says, or some sort of harmless malformation. Could it be a tumor, I ask? Maybe, anyway, I want you to get your bladder scoped. All right, I say. I will not be able to perform the procedure though, he says. No? No, I'm sorry, I was offered my dream job in the oncology unit at Rush, and today is my last day. Congratulations, I say. Thanks, he says, I am referring you to my colleague Dr. S. Okay. You'll like him, he adds.

(2001)

I Watch Bubbles Float Out of My Penis and Feel Like Liberace.

Dr. S. is smallish, well-coiffed, talkative. He reminds me of Teller, except for the talkative part. This is not a kidney stone, Dr. S. says. No? No. It could just be a defect of some kind, he says, but it could also be a tumor. We'll scope your kidneys and take a look. Don't worry about it, he says. It's probably nothing. Yeah? People don't get bladder cancer at your age, he adds. I have to go to the hospital. They don't scope you in the doctor's office. They give me local anesthesia and tell me I will be awake for the procedure. I'm not though. I fall asleep immediately. When I awake three hours later I'm freezing and hungry. They give me Lorna Doone cookies and say I cannot leave until I urinate. I don't want to stay, but I don't want to urinate either. I don't know what it will feel like, but I know it will be bad. I do urinate though. There is blood everywhere, and bubbles. I feel like Liberace. The scope finds nothing. Which is good, but for the pain in my back that won't go away. It's my kidneys apparently. They're bruised from the probing I'm told. I'm also told it will pass.

(2001)

The Pain In My Back Does Not Subside.

The pain in my back does not subside. I call Dr. S. several days later. Should I be worried about this back pain? I ask. No, it's normal. Really? Really. Ok. I'm glad you called though, he says. I catch my breath. No one is happy you called back on your own unless shit is going south. When we were probing your kidneys, he says, we did a wash just to see what might come up. A wash? I say. A wash, he says, and then we ran some tests. Right. You show a number of abnormal cells and they reflect a high likelihood of carcinoma, he says. Carcinoma, does that mean I have cancer? I ask. I don't know, maybe, I doubt it. But there could be something hidden in there that we missed, he says. Hidden? We need to do a biopsy of your bladder, he continues. Biopsy? We could have done it last time we were in there, but everything looked fine, he says. Okay. It's probably nothing, he adds, but you should come in. I'm supposed to go to Spain this week, can I still do that? I ask. Do you think so? he asks. Yes? Great, come in after that.

(2001)

I Go to Spain.

I go to Spain with my wife. We stalk Gaudi. We find out we are not pregnant though we were sure we were. We are sad. We drink beer. We eat cold potato pies. We try not to think about Cancer. We come home. I go back to the hospital and back to sleep. When I awake, I'm freezing. Again. This time though the pain is excruciating. I cannot bend. I cannot stand. I cannot bear to get dressed. And I will not urinate, but I do. It's bloody and paralyzing. They give me Vicodin and send me home.

(2001)

Night Sweats and Saltines.

I collapse into bed. I awake at 3:00am with night sweats. The muscle is being peeled off my back. Cramps undulate across my stomach. I take my Vicodin. Nothing happens. Nothing. Twenty minutes pass. Still nothing. I walk to the living room window. I watch the parking lot attendants behind our building move cars. But nothing happens. One hour passes. I eat a saltine and then another as I shuffle back and forth across the living room. The cramps subside. Another hour passes. The cramps return. It's been two hours and forty-five minutes. I want more Vicodin, but I have to wait three hours before I can take another one. I stare at the bottle. It stares back. I reach the three-hour mark. I rip the cap off the bottle. The cramps subside. I crawl into bed and curl up into a ball. Two hours later I need more Vicodin. And so it goes, all day long and into the night. (2001)

Aberrations.

It is morning. I cannot walk, or move. There is a band of pain I wear like a weight belt. I call Dr. S. He says it's possible that they perforated my bladder and that I should come in. I do. It's nothing. It turns out that the side effects of the Vicodin are mimicking the side effects of the surgery. The result is intense gas and cramps. Go cold turkey, and take these, Dr. S. says as he hands me some new pills. And the results of the biopsy? I ask. Nothing, it showed nothing. No tumors, no cancer, you're fine. But what about the blood and the murky IVP and the abnormal cells? I say. Aberrations, he says. All of that? I say. All of that. What are the next steps then? I ask. Get a physical in six months, he says, and get your blood checked and your urine tested. That's it? Yes. And I believe him. I do. But not fully. And not really. (2001)

I Drop My Pants.

I go in for a physical. Dr. W. is gone. He has moved his growing family back to New Jersey. Dr. L. has replaced him. He's tall, good looking, neatly dressed, and focused on me and my history. I tell him what's been going on and he doesn't like the sound of it. It doesn't jibe, too random, too many pieces that don't make sense. He calls Dr. S. They talk, he feels better. He tells me to drop my pants. He wants to check me for testicular cancer. I drop them my pants. I turn to my right. I cough. He squeezes something and it hurts. Have you noticed this before? he asks. No, what? I say. I don't know, one second, he says. He squeezes the spot again. It kills. Could be some extra skin, he says, could be a cyst. A cyst? Fuck me. It's probably nothing, he says, and even if it is a cyst, it could still be nothing. So that's good? Well, given your history, he continues, I would like you to get an ultrasound.
(2002)

My Balls Are Smeared With Cranberries.

I go get an ultrasound. I strip. It's cold in the room. It's cold on the table. The stuff they smear on my testicles looks like leftover cranberries the day after Thanksgiving. The young technician gets to work. I fall asleep. It's quiet. Peaceful.

Someone is talking to me. Hey man, dude, yo dude. It's the technician. What am I looking for man? I don't see anything here. It's a cyst, I say, it's supposed to be somewhere on the right side of my testicles. Well man there's nothing there, he says, you're cool. I talk to Dr. L. Good news, he says, there was nothing there. We had to check. And now? Come back next year for your annual physical.
(2002)

Wool Socks.

My baby son is sick with the flu. My wife is sick with the flu. I am not, but assume I will be soon. My lower back is sore. As the day progresses I cannot get warm. I pull on my wool socks and fleece pants, but nothing works. This continues long into the night. I spend the next day in bed napping. By dinner I feel fine, whatever it was has come and gone. I sleep like a baby that night. The next morning there is blood in my urine and lots of it. It continues all day and into the next. I make an appointment with Dr. L. He has a little less hair then last time I saw him. He's skinnier as well. Too skinny maybe. I wonder if he's ok, but I don't ask. What do you think is causing the blood? I do ask. I think this is a condition where the flu virus interferes with your kidney function, he says. Great, if you tell me that's what it is, I won't even bother to call you next time this happens, I say. Well, given your family history, he says, and your history I would feel better if you got a CAT Scan. Really? Really, I also want you to follow-up with your Urologist, he continues.

(2003)

A Cold, Hard Table.

I go in for a CAT scan. I am given two bottles of Barium. I am told to drink one immediately, and then the other in 20 minute intervals over the next hour. When I am done I am led into a room and asked to lie down on a cold, hard, metal table. I am slid into a cylindrical tube. Intermittently I am asked to hold my breath over the next twenty minutes. I do as they ask and then I am done.

(2003)

The Stone.

One week later my wife and I meet with an Urologist named Dr. T. Dr. T has sandy blonde hair and a limp handshake. He does not smile. We discuss my recent medical history. Dr. T. types everything I say into a computer. He never once looks away from the screen. I talk about the stabbing pain in my back, murky IVP's, and bladder biopsies. I have always thought these various maladies were due to kidney stones, I say. That possibility has always been dismissed, I continue. I'm looking at the results from your CAT Scan right now, he says. I can see a small stone in your right kidney that has been there for some time, he continues. Yeah? I say. I can also see several other ones growing in your left kidney, he adds. Really? I say. Really, it's right here, he says, tapping the computer screen with his right index finger. Could the one in the right kidney have been wedged there for the last four and a half years? I ask. Yes, he says. And could that explain the chronic lower back pain, the malformed cells and the blood in my urine? Yes, he says. Ok. Ok. So, can you treat it?" I ask. It's too small to treat, he says. I want you to change your diet and see whether or not you can break it down first, he continues. Ok. You shouldn't have this many kidney stones at your age though, he says. No? I also want to run a metabolic test on your urine and try to pinpoint the possible causes. Yeah? Yes, he says, walk over to the Center for Urology down the hall and they will set you up. Sounds great, I say. And it does. I'm ready to move on. If only it were that easy. You know, Dr. T. says, the blood in your urine seems disproportionate to the stone you have. Huh? We need to eliminate the possibility that there is a tumor in your bladder, he continues. Again? I ask. Yes, he says. But you won't need to do a Cystoscopy again will you? I ask. Yes, he says, we will. We will schedule it so the results from the metabolic test

are back at the same time, he continues.
(2003)

Easter Island.

The receptionist at the Center for Urology gives me two brown plastic containers. And two vials of preservatives. You will wake-up, she says, and urinate into one of these containers. You will continue to urinate in that container over the next 24 hours. You will then repeat that with the other container for the 24 hours following that. You will not need to refrigerate them, the preservatives will do the trick. I place the containers on the shelf in my bathroom overlooking the toilet. They loom there, like the Heads from Easter Island. They are stoic, strong, and beautiful, standing guard and offering greetings to the bathroom's visitors. Both containers come folded in on one side and slowly expand with each visit. I lug the semi-filled containers to the Center and turn them in along with a blood sample. The nurse gives me a copy of a special diet for people suffering from kidney stones. I need to cut out spinach. Who knew? So, the nurse says, you're seeing Dr. T. Yep. Not much of a personality, she says, but he's the best on kidney stones.
(2003)

I Yelp.

I go in for my Cystoscopy. I lay down naked on the table. The nurse comes in, doesn't say a word and starts pouring liquid Lydocaine into my penis. You know, I say, last time I did this they used the gel form to numb the tip of my penis. No reaction. Any reason you choose to use the liquid form? I continue. It's more effective this way baby, she says. I like being called baby. Still. Really, I say, because I'm not feeling very numb. You're number than you think, she says. She smiles and leaves. Dr. T. comes in. He walks over to me and without a comment he inserts the tube into my penis. I feel the tube sliding along every step of the way. It's too big by a half. There is a pinch. I grimace. The pinching sensation does not pass. I grab the sheet. I let out a yelp. I have never yelped. You will feel a pinch as we pass through your sphincter, Dr. T. says. He's done. The procedure has lasted a few minutes at best. Dr. T. pauses for a moment and then removes the tube. No tumors, he says. And the results of metabolic test? I ask. They didn't get here in time, he says, call me in one week and we'll talk. He reaches out to shake my hand. And with that he's gone.

(2004)

Blood Vessels.

I call Dr. T. one week later. I have started to see blood in my urine again. Why are you trying to reach me? he asks. You told me to call you and follow-up on the metabolic test, I say. And I know the Cystoscopy looked good, but I have blood in my urine again. Any concerns there? Yes, he says, we may need to do another IVP. And then he moves on. You don't drink enough fluids, he says. Drink two cups of water when you wake-up, a quart during the day. And two more cups before you go to bed. Lemonade is also good, as is orange juice and grapefruit juice. You also have too many Oxcidents in your urine, he says. Oxcidents build kidney stones. Cut out tea, chocolate and raspberries. Do you have a copy of the special diet we've written-up? Yeah, I do, I say. Good, take a look at it. He has not mentioned the blood in my urine. By the way, he says, in terms of the blood in your urine, everything looks clean. So, it may be that the kidney stone that's wedged in my right kidney is causing it? I ask. Yeah maybe, he says, but it could also be a malformed blood vessel. Really. Yes. And what does that mean exactly? I say. It's kind of like how other people get bloody noses. Really? I say. Yes. Is it just a coincidence then that I may have both a malformed blood vessel in my kidneys and stones? Yes, he says. And how do you treat that exactly? I ask. We would cauterize it, he says. Dear god.

What I suggest, he says, is that next time you see blood in your urine, you call me immediately. We will do another Cystoscopy and look for the source, he continues. Another Cystoscopy, I say. Yes. Ok, I say. That's it for now then. Ok, thanks. Bye.

(2004)

I Pass the Stone.

I drink more water. When I wake-up. When I go to bed. And all day long. One day I am at work. I am in the bathroom. I pass the stone. Just like that. Like magic. No pain. Just a weirdness. A push and something jagged and crystalline is staring at me like a far away star come to Earth. No escape. No hubris. No attempts at greatness. It is just a thing that was stuck somewhere, and now is not. I pluck it out of the toilet. I place it in a baggy. I show it Dr. T. That's it, he says.

(2004)

END OF STORY

Here is what we know: we plan to find out that we are pregnant while we are lounging in the decadence that is San Sebastian, Spain.

This is actually not much of a plan, and we know that, because we also know that you cannot plan these things, not really.

However, we do know that it will happen, because we want it to be true, because we were once at a party where we learned about this magical place called San Sebastian, and now that we are finally able to go, we have decided that when we get there we will be pregnant, period, end of story.

Again, that's not much of a plan, and maybe I should back-up for a moment anyway.

My wife Debbie and I are at a party at some long ago

co-worker's loft in some Chicago neighborhood whose location is now lost to me.

The crowd is young and cool, lots of short hair and black T-shirts, and they're doing what young, cool people do so well—looking good in lofts while drinking craft beers, talking about training runs and listening to the Tragically Hip.

The co-worker's husband is from Dublin, Ireland, and one of his high school friends is there with his striking curly-haired Irish-American wife. We are happy just to listen as the high school friend talks, it doesn't matter about what, his voice is lovely, all lilt and whiskey saturated.

So there we are, hanging on his every word as he regales us with stories of his endless travels and we try to discern whether he might be at least distantly related to Larry Mullens, Jr.

We are struck that this guy has lived a certain kind of life. He has done things, and been places, and we really have not, not as a couple anyway. We are still building a life together, and while on the one hand we feel like we've had few adventures in comparison to him, on the other, merely speaking to him leaves us feeling like the possibility of adventure is right there if we just reach out and grab it.

"If you could tell someone where to go, just one place, where would that be?" Debbie asks him.

"That's easy," he says, "San Sebastian, Spain, there's

nowhere else like it."

And that's that. We don't need to know anything else. We don't even need to know why he thinks this. We apparently needed a place to go, and though we didn't know this when we left the house, we do now, just like that.

The cool story would be how we went home that night, dropped everything, booked our trip, and were soon having a threesome with Larry Mullens, Jr. under the ocean spray that endlessly cascades over San Sebastian's horseshoe beachfront.

But that isn't what happened.

Instead, my father got sick, cancer sick, eighteen months to live sick, any trip of any real length, didn't seem possible sick, and for the most part we didn't go anywhere that didn't look like a cancer ward or my parent's house until my father passed away.

Instead of ocean spray, there was the drip, drip, drip of IV's, and instead of Sangria there was talk of Thalidomide, and a string of blurry days with him that never seemed like anything other than borrowed time despite our fervent desires for some kind of news that would tell us everyone was wrong.

Not that it was all death, there was life as well, or the idea of life, as Debbie and I started talking about the baby we would someday have.

The presence of this still unborn child in our lives was

something both real and far away, and it existed in a kind of parallel universe to that of my father's illness; first lingering there like a ghost, and then gaining a sense of realness when the sadness around my father's loss was replaced by the need to create new life.

Before there could be a baby though, I needed an adventure, something travel, real life, and electric.

Debbie did not.

She was ready to move forward even as I was ready to run away, and with her blessing, I ran to Italy, gone, no death, no wife, no nothing, but Jackson Pollack, The David and Caravaggio.

Then Debbie changed her mind.

She wanted the baby and the adventure, and we decided that not only would we start trying, but that we would learn our baby was something real when we got to San Sebastian. Going there had been delayed, but now we could go, and it was going to be magic, we felt we had earned it. As family folklore has it, when my parents had been married for seven years they decided they had the proof they needed that they were going to stay together and they traveled through Europe for several months. When they got to Italy my mother was certain she was pregnant. When they got to Spain she was told she was not, and she was crushed. But when they got home, they found that she was pregnant after all, and had been all along. The doctor was wrong, she was right, and there was me, or there would be soon.

And so it goes.

For some chunk of our life most of us do everything we can not to get pregnant, while still hoping to have as much sex as possible. We are careful, mostly, but not always, because there are so many things that impact our better judgment, alcohol, watching *Fatal Attraction*, poor impulse control; and so many things that can go wrong regardless, ripped condoms, missed birth control pills and the act of pulling out that isn't quite pulling out at all.

But then some of us decide that we are done doing everything we've been doing to avoid having a child, and it's amazing how hard it is, or how hard it feels, to make it happen when so much now has to go right, and so many things are working against you, including, but not limited to luck, timing, and your own body, because any or all of that is happy to fuck things up.

Which takes us to San Sebastian, and how in all of our death infused, magical thinking, we have made a plan, not that you can plan on anything, not dead father's, not babies being born, and not even as it turns out, my own cancer scare, because while we are making all of these plans, a shadow appears on my kidney, and I am peeing blood and the doctors just don't know why.

Nor do they care that my father has recently died from

some rare form of cancer that people know so little about and we think we deserve a break, or that we plan to have a baby because we've earned that, or even that we are leaving in one week to go to Spain where we will find out that this baby is a very real thing, because they definitely don't care about our plans.

They do however, sort of care about the incredible pain I'm experiencing in my lower back after they scope my kidney, because this pain is so excruciating I'm not clear how I can go to Spain at all.

But even that, they don't care all that much about.

"Do you really think I'm okay to fly?" I ask my urologist.

"You are fine to fly," he says, "this will pass."

"And so that's it?" I ask.

"Not exactly," he says, "when we washed out your kidneys, we did find some oddly shaped cells, and so we're going to need to biopsy your bladder when you get back."

"And that's because you think I have cancer?" I ask.

"We don't know," he said. "It's probably nothing. Go enjoy yourself."

Which we try to do, despite the rainy, overcast, skies that greet us in San Sebastian, the waves that constantly crash over the boardwalk, making it nearly impossible to walk anywhere, the wind that somehow swirls in all directions at once and the restaurants that never seem to be open.

Still, we are there, we have made it. The room is lovely. The horseshoe shaped shore is in place. And everything is going according to plan. We are where we are destined to be, and there are no IV's, dead dads, or scoped kidneys, just a biopsy awaiting us, which we will choose to ignore, so we can lose ourselves in the baby we are certain to find out that we are having.

Again, all of which is a fine plan, except that on our first morning there we wake-up to coffee, fresh baked rolls, the waves pounding the boardwalk beneath our window, and the fact that there is no baby, and no magic, just dashed dreams, more loss, and the realization that you can't will a baby into being any more than you can will your father to stay alive when nothing tells you he actually will.

Which leaves us where exactly?

Nowhere, that's where, well, besides a bar, drinking cold beer, eating cold fish sandwiches and going home.

Which I suppose is a certain kind of ending to the story, at least the particular story we had written out of hopes and dreams and grief before there was even a story to write.

That doesn't mean the story can't have a different kind of ending though, because that's the thing about plans, you can make other ones when you have to. And so in that vein, a coda if you will, though with your permission, I am going to offer you two.

We are home, we are sad and I still need to have a biopsy.

When I wake-up the morning of the biopsy, I realize I don't know how long it will be before I can go for a run, but I do know I have an hour before we leave and I am off. Which is cool, or not, depending on whether you are Debbie, or me.

"Dude," Debbie says when I get home, "you went for a run?"

"I know I'm having surgery, and maybe it was dumb, but I had to go, I'm sorry," I say.

"I don't care about your surgery," she says, "but I'm ovulating, you're running and we need to leave in 30 minutes. Let's go."

Let's go indeed.

And now for coda number two.

A month later I am on a plane, the sun is rising over the Pacific Ocean, my kidneys are pain free and there is no cancer. There are no answers, but no cancer, which is nice because you can't plan on learning you're cancer-free any more than you can plan on anything else.

As I sit there, I think about my father and all the sunsets he will never again see, what it means to plan for things that may never be, and how sometimes we search for magic in places otherwise unknown to us.

I'm also thinking about how much of that is past

already, how quickly we move on to the next things in life, and then the things after that, because that's what life is, endless disappointments, and some triumphs, yet always, and inevitably, we make new plans and we move forward regardless.

For a moment, it's amazingly still, the quiet pounding my head from all sides, but then I hear a baby cry out from somewhere behind me, and I take this as a sign of not what might have been, but what is yet to come.

Because here's the thing, that morning as my biopsy loomed, and questions of life and death swirled around us like those winds in San Sebastian, it happened. We made a baby, and while that baby is no more than four weeks old, and no more than a blip on a screen, there is a baby, and magic, and if we have learned nothing about making plans, much less how anything works, we at least know that sometimes, our stories, and plans, end, and begin, just like this.

IRA GLASS WANTS TO HIT ME

I do not consider myself to be a stalker. Nor do I think of myself as much of a sycophant. I am a bit of a star-fucker though and at one time anyway a lover of anything and everyone associated with Ira Glass and the radio show *This American Life*.

It once seemed to me that my writing was perfect for the show, but you don't have to take my word for it, many people told me so.

No, you wouldn't know them, but you can trust me.

It also seemed to me that under the right circumstances Ira Glass and I could be great friends, and I knew this in the same way that so many of my single female friends know that they are perfect for John Cusack.

How do they know this?

I think you know the answer to that.

But how does one get a piece on the show? Or even meet Ira Glass who I understand rests in a cryogenically sealed chamber between shows?

I imagine one could lurk outside the studio or Ira's home, though again please note that I am not a stalker, and that the charges to that affect that may, or may not, have once been filed by NPR's legal office here in Chicago did not stick.

One could also submit their work to the show, which I have done, but how well does one's actual work reflect their wit, timing, and ability to move the public to tears, joy, and maybe even arousal in the space of one sentence?

Not well, not my work anyway.

Enter Jennifer.

I should probably mention, that all names in this piece have been changed to protect the innocent, but one, and if this bothers anyone referenced therein please feel free to call me and we can talk about it, especially if you are Ira Glass, and by the way, if you are, I'm am absolutely waiting by my phone.

So, Jennifer is on a plane. Jennifer is sexy. Smart. And funny. Jennifer meets one of *This American Life*'s producers, let's call him Steve, which is not his actual name, but I digress, because you know that already, and Steve invites her to watch a taping of the show any time she wants. Jennifer in turn invites a number of us from the office to join her, and its game on.

What to wear though?

Black t-shirt and a blazer, something corduroy?

What?

Are we thinking more Rivers Cuomo or David Sedaris?

Tricky.

I settle on a rumpled blue v-neck sweater, a green hounds tooth dress shirt and baggy jeans—confident, but casual, eye-catching, but not distracting.

I feel good, comfortable, Ira has no idea what's coming.

Jennifer and I go to the studio on a Friday night and Steve is very friendly, showing us around and seating us for the taping.

Ira, of course, is majestic as he does his interlocutor thing.

Jon Langford from the Mekons shows up.

And people applaud uproariously.

It's all very cool, but Ira has to re-tape some sections of the show and so beyond a quick hello we fail to get any quality time with him.

Is this frustrating?

Sure it is, to be so close to your dream and see it slowly slipping between your fingers, it's crushing really.

But then we are invited to join the staff for drinks and we are told that Ira may come by. My plan at this point is simple—when Ira arrives I will ply him with drinks and so charm him with my witty banter and storytelling that he will pray to all that is holy that I am a writer who can write for the show, and then when he finds out I am one, it will be the beginning of a long, loving and fruitful relationship.

That's the plan anyway.

As we await Ira's presence I ask Steve some subtle, yet pointed questions about those who write for the show.

"So, how does someone like get a piece on the show?" I say. "What's the secret?"

"Writing for the show is a lot different than just writing a story," Steve says, "there's a whole different rhythm."

"Right," I say, not clear what that means, "so, when does Ira get here?"

Steve doesn't respond to that, but he doesn't need to, Ira has entered the bar.

I linger on the periphery of the conversation Steve is having with Jennifer, and try to worm my way into Ira's group.

"I'm just worried that I peaked way too soon," Ira is saying, "that this is it for me, you know?"

The group stands there silently hanging on Ira's every word.

I hope he will turn to me though, maybe the usual hangers-on have heard this lament before, but I haven't and I want to be there for him.

I try to seize the moment, carpe diem and all that.

"Hey man," I say, "let's say you have peaked, it's already quite a legacy, more than most people can hope to accomplish."

Ira doesn't respond, instead he just stares at me though through his clunky black glasses.

It doesn't matter that he's silent though, I can tell he needs me to be his anchor, steering him through this storm of self-doubt and questionable mixed metaphors.

"Fine," I say, "let's forget what I just said, but let's not forget that there are a number of examples of people with a series of peaks, Jack Johnson, moving from hunky professional surfer to hunky singer, Jim Brown from football legend to legendary actor, and what of Jodie Foster, she went from the kid in the original Coppertone ad to child star to Oscar winning actress and sometime director."

Ira is silent.

He runs his fingers through his magnificent wavy black hair.

I wish I were those fingers.

Let's pause here for a moment.

When I later relate this story to my therapist he will say that I was showing-off here and that I was acting needy.

Okay, he didn't call me needy, but he did use the phrase "showing-off," which I interpreted at least in part as needy.

And I was, both, in that I was hoping to make an impression, and wanting something so nakedly I was willing to embarrass myself, which sometimes works with the right person at the right time.

Sometimes.

We can un-pause now.

"Jodie Foster was not the kid in the Coppertone ad," Ira practically shouts at me.

This is tough.

I fight my need to be a know-it-all one-day at time, it's a lifelong battle, but I embrace it. I want to be a better person and the fact that I am pretty much always right is beside the point.

Still, as good a job as I do, it is hard to keep my composure in the face of those who choose not to fight the good fight themselves.

I want to push back, but part of my recovery is striving not to prove others wrong, and in this case, its Ira, who I don't want to alienate, he is the gatekeeper of all I hold sacred.

"You know, you might be right," I say. "I think I've heard otherwise, but who knows."

That's fairly polite I think. He will appreciate that. He's Ira Glass.

—

It may be important to note here, that when I say things such as, "you may be right," I probably don't think you are, but I'm really trying not to be a dick, which may in fact make me a dick regardless.

Regardless, I really don't want to sound like a know it all, and I am equally happy to avoid confrontation over things that carry such little import.

And sometimes that even works.

Sometimes.

"You're wrong," Ira says, "and I will bet you all the money in my wallet that you're wrong."

Ira starts rifling through his wallet and comes up with seven dollars.

"I will bet you seven dollars," he says.

"I don't want to bet you dude," I say. "It's cool, really."

At this point, Ira looks away and moves onto another conversation.

This is not going well.

Still, I have met Ira Glass and he certainly must appreciate how deftly I moved us out of this potentially dangerous situation, diffusing all tension between us, while remaining cordial and light on my feet.

Don't guests of the show need to possess such talents?

Ira turns back to me.

He looks somewhat intense.

"You're wrong about Jodie Foster," he says.

I have done all I can do to be cool and not care about this, but I can't hold back any more, my chance at someday writing for *This American Life*, be damned.

"Sorry Ira," I say, "but you're wrong, totally wrong, deal with it."

Ira pauses.

I think he wants to hit me.

I try to imagine what it's like getting hit by Ira Glass.

Pretty cool that, right?

Over time people have asked me if I was disappointed by this exchange, and whether Ira becoming so unhinged over Jodie Foster and my sad attempt at hero worship has left me doubting my love for him and what he has built.

It's quite the opposite really.

It turns he's actually human and weird, and if I was never going to write for the show anyway, it's a story now, and I want to tell stories regardless of the platform.

Still, was it weird? Of course it was.

Ira's girlfriend suddenly materializes from the crowd, and she's quite foxy.

"What's going on," she says fixing her eyes on him, "are you claiming yet again that you know something that isn't actually true?"

"No," Ira says sheepishly, "but this guy says Jodie Foster was the kid in the Coppertone ad and there's no way."

"Wrong, she was, everyone knows that," the girlfriend says exhaustively.

She's clearly done this before.

Maybe after every show there's someone like me there, and maybe after every show something goes awry because of it.

"Fine," he says and then he hands me the seven dollars.

"Ira I don't want your money," I say even as I visualize it framed on my wall.

He turns away and we don't speak again. I've lost my chance. I shift back to Steve.

"So, seriously man, how do you get something on the show?" I say.

"Just submit dude," Steve says.

And so I do, again and again, all the while dreaming about the next time Ira and I are out together, drinking beers, talking about my growing role on the show and laughing about Jodie Foster and all of the things we are willing to do for the things we think we love.

HERE WE ARE

Please don't say anything," my mother says.

Dave, the guy we dealt with at the cemetery when we buried my father will not send my mother the receipt reflecting that she has paid for my father's plot, as well as hers, and this despite the fact that she has asked him for it repeatedly, and he has said it's on the way.

The need for the receipt is a practical one certainly, it is proof that my father is really dead and that some day she might be as well.

But the receipt is also an anchor in the midst of the chaos that is my father's loss, something to focus on, to hold onto, something concrete in a world now full of memories, emotions, and jolting associations with the places they've been, and might have gone, and all those late night conversations, full of coffee, and passion, and the stickiness which kept them together, and happy.

I should say, that when I say, that Dave *will not* send my mother the receipt, that's not truly accurate, there is no dispute, or unpaid bills, he's just choosing not to send it, doing so is not urgent for him, and he's on to the next thing.

Which has upset my mom, which has upset me, and here we are.

"Please don't say anything," my mother says.

I'm going to see her the next day, she wants calm, and she doesn't want to burden me, and she didn't tell me this story because she secretly wants me to do something about it. She told me the story because my dad is dead and she would have told him, but she can't.

"Hey Dave," I say into his voice mail minutes later, "it's Ben Tanzer. My mother says that you haven't sent her the receipt you promised to send her. I'm visiting her tomorrow, and if she hasn't received it by noon when I get there, I'm going to drive to your office and kick the shit out of you. After that, I'm going to kick the shit out of anyone else who happens to be there. Thanks, man."

And then I hang-up.

I remained calm and I spoke excessively slow, consciously trying to land each word and beat like a punch

Now I'm shaking and cold.

And my heart is pounding.

But even with all of that, I have also started to bounce

on my toes as I picture punching Dave in his perfect fucking weatherman face until he starts to cry, and I begin to
hope, just a little, that maybe Dave won't respond and I will
have to act on my threat.

My chest starts to ache.

It starts off feeling like a bruise, but then begins to
spasm as well, the muscle constricting, then not, my whole
body in its grip.

"What did you do," my mother says calling me not
five minutes later, "the receipt just came through on my
fax machine."

"Nothing," I say.

So, we were faced with a situation, not a major one certainly, not life and death, but still a major situation for us,
that wasn't getting settled by being polite.

It was settled by the threat of violence, not even an
actual act, just the suggestion of it.

What am I to take from that, and what does it tell me,
that in the moment I was fully prepared to back it up?

I was going to get in a car, drive six hours, get out of
that car and hurt someone. And yes, it involved my mother,
and yes, I was enraged, but it seemed so rational to me,
though not even merely rational, but logical, and then not
even just logical, but weirdly triumphant, and fun, and this
despite the muscles contracting across my chest.

And if I can even begin answer this question for myself, how should I explain any of this to my children?

There was a time when one of the boys was being bullied by a kid so incessantly that I pictured punching the kid myself, though if not him, his father then.

The urge was driven by a kind of impotence, a festering anger that my child was suffering, and the desire to make it end in the only way that seemed to make sense when nothing else seemed to be working.

My son sought to avoid the kid, sitting at different tables, and not getting-up to sharpen his pencil when the other kid was doing so himself.

He couldn't always avoid him, however.

Some of the bullying was verbal, stupid stuff, kid bullshit, and my son got really good at talking his way out of situations, turning the other boy's words against him.

And so often that would be enough, the other kid too flabbergasted to respond.

Sometimes though, the kid would shove him, emboldened, angered, or too frustrated to walk away, and when that happened, my son would say to us, "but I did everything right, I tried to avoid him, and when I couldn't, I tried to talk my way out of it, and I got shoved anyway. What am I supposed to do?"

What could I say to him, that sometimes you will do

everything right, like pay for your funeral plot in a timely manner and merely seek your receipt, or avoid bullies, and stay calm, but that some people are just damaged assholes, and maybe it's better to just learn that now.

Which is more or less what I said to him, but that doesn't mean it explains anything about anything, or maybe I should say, that while such an explanation may serve him in the long run, what about now—how is he supposed to deal with feelings that are all over the place, and have no logical means for being managed?

What should he do with that, when we have let him down, the school has let him down and what should work is not working?

What do you do then?

Nothing?

Maybe that's the answer sometimes, but not for me.

"Why don't you shove him back," I finally said, "just once, hard, knock him over, it will all be done after that, no bully wants to be pushed back, promise."

He looked stunned, bemused even.

"Are you kidding," he responded, "that's against the rules."

Apparently, the fact that the other kid broke the rules first doesn't matter, my son lives in a world where you don't do that, even if some people clearly do.

And so he didn't shove him, and it mostly all went

away, but there are times, even still, when he will say, "My dad told me to shove someone."

He's incredulous when he says, but so am I, because anxieties aside, he seems to be growing-up in a different world than I did.

My father fought as a kid, though maybe it's more accurate to say that he grew-up rough, or that he was delinquent, that he thought this was cool, and that he regaled us with stories to ensure that we thought so too.

For example, the time he and his friends got into a fight in Chinatown while buying fireworks and ended-up throwing the firecrackers at the guys they bought them from.

Or how they would pour hot tar in paper bags during long summer days and then throw them onto the windows of the police cars below, before running from roof to roof to make their escape.

Even that he nicknamed himself the "Rock," because he wanted everyone to know just how tough he was.

And you should see the photos of him then, the white T-shirts, with the rolled up sleeve holding his pack of cigarettes, the ducktail.

Or just talk to his younger brothers who still talk about his tough guy ways in tones one could only describe as reverent.

It was all real, as were the fights he got into even as an adult, mostly verbal, but physical too, like the time he bragged to me about the altercation he got into with the local Tai Chi expert—let that sink in for a moment—which ended when my father hit him with an easel.

Or, this story of Oedipal strife, which he was always happy to repeat:

"So, you came in one morning when you were little wearing a cape and carrying two swords, and you challenged me to fight you for your mother's hand."

"And," I said, the first time he told me it anyway, "what happened?"

"What happened," he said, yes, incredulously, "I kicked your ass."

So there is that, and the fighting I engaged in to be just like him, mostly winning, but losing as well, a string of battles with school bullies, because one, I wouldn't back down, from anyone, ever, that's so not tough, and two, seeing people get bullied enraged me, and I gladly inserted myself into those fights any chance I could get.

One of the highlights of those battles was my beating-up the much bigger Robert English, who was known for both tormenting our smaller contemporaries, as well as pouring snow cones into mailboxes, but who succumbed to me when I got him in a headlock, flipped him onto his back, and choked him until he turned red and spit phlegm everywhere.

A move I learned from my father of course.

All of which sounds like bragging, and it is, though it is also tinged with the embarrassment of knowing that while I want the world to be a less violent place, that I believe violence begets violence, and that I really want my children to be better versions of me, I still associate being a man with being tough, that being tough sometimes involves violence, and that I wouldn't mind if both of my sons remained the incredibly loving and sensitive boys they are, but still wish they might still be willing to shove someone, when appropriate, and needed.

After I was randomly assaulted that one day in New York City, I was in a bar in my upstate New York hometown and a guy I knew from high school said, "I would have never let that happen to me."

It was stated as a matter of fact and wholly judgmental, and whether he was correct or not, it didn't matter, my reaction was shame.

How could I let this guy hit me?

Couldn't I have gotten away?

And if not, how didn't I fight back?

I hated myself for not doing something more, and I still do. But that feeling didn't surprise me, what did surprise me, was the fear, or more accurately my reaction after that to shouts in the night and sudden movements, shadows, and aggression directed my way in bars, stores, trains, everywhere.

The initial reaction is always one of fury, heart pounding, a surge of adrenaline, and then the desire to fight. The next is to pummel the person where that shout, stance, or shadow originates from, all of which runs its course when I begin to feel the euphoria that accompanies the sure victory I am picturing in my head.

All of which is to say that when I threatened Dave the cemetery guy, I felt like I was channeling my father, but I know now that I was also accessing the endlessly pent-up rage, shame and trauma that lingers just below the surface ever since the assault, until its triggered anyway, and washing over me like a wave, easy to feel, but hard to embrace, much less re-direct.

Years ago, I was home for a moment. I was heading off to a new life in San Francisco, but stopped upstate first to visit my parents and make some money for the move.

One day the temp agency I signed-up with assigned me to a local warehouse where windows were stored until being shipped-out.

The two regular warehouse guys ignored me all day, going about their business, talking shit and doing whatever they were going to do whether a temporary guy was there or not.

Near the end of the day the bigger of the two guys started to tell the other guy about a fight at one of the local bars the night before, in which a smaller dude had taken on a much bigger one.

The other guy was hanging on every word, and so was I.

Suddenly the bigger guy said, "Size doesn't matter, it's all about toughness, take Ben Tanzer over there, he beat-up Robert English and that guy was way bigger than him."

The two of them finally looked at me.

"You beat up Robert English?" the smaller guy asked me.

"I guess I did," I replied, "it was a long time ago."

"Cool," he said.

After that, they went back to their conversation and ignored me for the rest of their shift.

I still remember it like it was yesterday.

DOWNBOUND TRAIN

I am in high school and I am required to take a creative writing class. We keep a journal and we are expected to write in it every day.

Some days we receive prompts, such as "write something inspired by your favorite poem," and I choose a piece by Ogden Nash, or the Eagles song "Hotel California." Other days we are expected to write entries based on something that has inspired us in our daily lives, and one time I quote myself from a college application essay I am writing about "personal transformation."

One day though, I write a short story inspired by the Bruce Springsteen song "Downbound Train." In the song, a man loses his job and then his girl. It is intended as a pointed, and poignant, commentary on the recessionary 1980's, and the failure of America to support the working class.

In my homage, however, which is simply titled "Joe," it becomes something else. While Joe also loses his job and his girl, there is no rumination, or political intention, instead, the pressure builds in Joe's head until he decides to blow his brains out with a shotgun. He doesn't die though, despite the graphic descriptions I added of the gray matter and pieces of skull wedged in the wall behind him. Instead Joe feels a wind blow through his face, which is followed by a sense of relief, as the pressure in his head finally lifts.

Joe is amazed about how good he feels, how clear his thinking is and how much promise the world now holds for him.

And with that, he goes out for a beer.

"You never think about death?" my now wife, then girlfriend, Debbie asked me shortly after we first met.

"No, why would I?" I replied.

"Because you're worried about what the world will look like without you in it and whether anyone will notice you're gone regardless?" she said.

"No, sorry, never," I said.

And I meant it.

What does it feel like before you step off of a ledge? What is that moment like? Do you teeter or plunge? Is it a culmination of steps, moments of constant despair and pain leading to that moment? Or is it impulsive, sudden and volatile, grabbed with ferocity? What does it sound like after that step? Do you feel the wind in your face? Do you wonder if in fact you can float, or fly?

I thought about all of this when the author Ned Vizzini leapt to his death while home visiting his family on the East Coast, a place that was ostensibly safe for him, a harbor, but in this case, and at this time, was not. Was it easier for him to jump while visiting a place he knew and had roots in? And was it easier for him to know that his wife and child wouldn't have to find him because they were home on the West Coast? That it would all happen at a distance, thus not quite as real for them, removing the ongoing reminders that it happened where they live, even while being no less jolting, or painful. Can the victim of suicide even clearly think through these things? Is it possible that this may be the only moment they feel they've been able to clearly think in some time? Or is this kind of thinking only available to those left behind?

I don't know the answers to any of these questions, and I didn't know Ned Vizzini. I also don't know how often he thought about his death, or whether the possibility of it seemed like a gift. Not an end to life, but an end to what seemed impossible to him, living how he was living and had been for so long. But I did listen to an interview with him not so long before he died, where he joked about death constantly, and I wondered later, whether that was his way of coping, and distancing himself from his past attempts at suicide, or whether these comments were the seedlings of what was to come.

I don't know suicide either, not the hold that the idea of it must have on your brain once it clenches, or at least I didn't until Ned Vizzini took his life, and I had to re-order my thinking about all of that.

"Oh no," my friend's mother says, her face contorting, then collapsing, into something almost too sad to look at, as she covers her mouth and steps away from the phone in the kitchen where we are sitting.

I am twelve years old and have never in my life seen a face like that.

"What?" my friend, her son, says, as we stare at her.

"Phil is dead, they found him hanging off of his back porch," she replies as she begins to collect herself, her face returning to its normal dimensions.

"He killed himself?" my friend asks.

The quiet lingers there in the air as his mother pauses, and then squares her shoulders.

"What? No, they say he was playing with a noose, for fun, and it was an accident," she replies sternly, back in control, before walking out of the room, the conversation over.

Phil was the first suicide I knew, though I really didn't know him. He was a year older than me and he was a god—the best athlete in our school, with the hottest girl-friend, and the coolest friends. None of which I had, all of which I wanted. I only spoke to him once, by the side of the track. He was putting on his running shoes and he wished me luck in my race. It was a recognition, and an affirmation that I existed, but that was it. Then we were both off to our respective events, and soon after that he was dead.

It was called an accident, but I can't imagine anyone believed it was an accident. Regardless, it was also an event that no adult ever mentioned in my presence again. No teachers, no counselors, no parents, not mine or anyone else's, no one. Maybe no one knew what to say. Or maybe it was summer, and so maybe none of us were any-where anyone in authority could gather us to speak to. Then again, what do you say when the most popular kid in school hangs himself? It gets better? Because it does, we know that as adults, mostly, usually, but what if the kid who killed himself already represents the better to so many of us. What do you say then?

And what do I say then about Ned, and my inces-sant ruminations about his death? Ned is someone, who was open about his struggles, and who also represented a certain kind of better as well—famous friends, television

work, best-selling books, movie options, and both the recognition, and affirmation, that his books meant something
to a large number of readers. Any or all of which so many
of us want, though even some small taste of any of that
would suffice.

There is nothing I can say to shed greater light on Phil
or Ned's death, but there is a connection between these
two suicides for me, something personal and small. Like
Phil before him, Ned seemed to have what I really want.
But what does that mean? One thing it means is that I have
to admit that despite what I said to Debbie when we first
met, it isn't true that I never think about death. I think,
about Phil all of the time, his smile, how cool he was, our
one conversation, what happened, and why, and what he
might have become. I also think about another kid from
my neighborhood who hung himself not long after Phil.
That kid had not been as cool as Phil, or good-looking, he
didn't have a hot girlfriend. He would have been considered a "burn-out" in the parlance of the times. But he was
the king of PAC-Man, which was cool in its own way, and
then he was dead, found by a friend of mine, hanging from
a tree in his backyard.

I've been thinking about their suicides for over thirty
years now, the triggers coming often, and they crush me in
the process. River Phoenix's death especially, which wasn't
a suicide, not exactly, but it was something just like one,

or David Foster Wallace, Ned, Robin Williams, though any loss of anyone too soon will get me ruminating about those earlier ones.

It may be more accurate than to say that over the years I never thought about my own death. Or more specifically, taking my own life, that yes, I thought about death all of the time, it's just that I only thought about other people's deaths. Which is actually a lot like thinking about death, just called another name. Which might be a defense, or a deflection, but I don't know, I don't.

When I heard Ned had killed himself I was profoundly sad, and what I did know, is that I had already been feeling bad for some time, though I wasn't sure why. And what I now definitely know, is that his death didn't offer me any insights into why I felt as I did at the time, but it did suggest to me that there was a way to rid myself of the feeling I could not shake or unwrap from my brain. Suicide as an option would only later become clearer, though I don't know whether that is because I wouldn't allow myself to identify it for what it was.

What I knew, is that I had been feeling despondent for days, or maybe weeks. It wasn't always present, but it was lurking, waiting for me for when I slowed down, took a break, wasn't working or chasing kids, watching *Breaking Bad*, hadn't gone running, or was tired. What I also know, is that I wasn't sure how to shake it, or address this feeling that I couldn't begin to name in the first place.

The despondency I felt passed, fitfully at first. The mood lifted, and the feeling became a memory, and a ghost that had drifted off into the past. This didn't answer the why though, and even with a clearer head, and lighter mood, I wasn't sure what had gone down, or what had prompted it.

It was then that I listened to another interview with another writer, this one about suicide itself, and the expert talked about many things that resonated with me, but none more than the idea that one cause for suicide is the victim's need for affirmation. It was only then that the origins of the despondency I had felt became clear to me, and the why became illuminated.

My novel *Orphans* had been released in the fall. It had gotten kind reviews early on from major publications, a first for me, and I was sure it was the start of something. But soon there was nothing, and that's the thing with books, whatever is or is not, eventually stops. It's gradual at first, but soon no one is reading or talking about them. It's hard enough with any book, but I was hoping for more after those reviews—calls from agents, options, something. But it didn't happen and there's nothing one can do to control it.

Is it selfish and shallow of me to feel this way? Yes, of course it is.

And am I embarrassed to feel despondent over op-portunities that didn't materialize when there are so many horrible and violent things happening all the time? Unbe-lievably so.

But did I want more anyway? I did.

And did I now see how much the lack of perceived affirmation for *Orphans* left me feeling so despondent. I did not, not at first, not at all.

Why is this important? It isn't for the wider world, but it is for me.

I had another book out as I started processing all of this, *Lost in Space*, there has been another one since, and hopefully there will be others. I will want things all over again, and I know they may not happen, and so I must be prepared for the inevitable dark shroud that will wrap itself around my brain. I must also remind myself that things will change, that I will feel better, that Ned, and even Phil, seemingly had all of what I want, but that it wasn't enough, and that most importantly, I haven't always told those around me, much less myself, the truth about how I feel.

There is this young guy, he is wearing a black T-shirt and jeans, his hair is cut short, and he seems happy. It's sunny out, placid. The young man walks-up to a police officer who has his back turned to him as he talks to some other people on the sidewalk. The young man is clearly focused on the police officer's gun and I'm not surprised when he removes it from the officer's holster. He takes a moment to admire the pearl handle, which is gleaming in the sun, and seems odd for the kind of gun I expect the officer to have. No one seems bothered that the young guy has taken the gun, and I soon realize that he plans to shoot himself with it. I also realize that I know this young man because he is me, and I become alarmed that I want to shoot myself. I am also equally relieved however, that I know I am dreaming, and unlikely to have to watch myself die, because everyone knows that you never see yourself die in a dream. I am surprised then when I aim the gun at my face and pull the trigger. Except that I don't die, but instead feel the universe blow though my head and beyond as I find myself hurtling through space and time. Or maybe I do, because maybe this is what death looks like, a blowing wind, and then nothing, something that didn't occur to me when I awoke this morning, only now, as I am writing this down and adding it to this essay that is already in motion.

If I submitted my high school story "Joe" today, it would call for an intervention of some kind.

A school counselor would be contacted. My parents would be asked to come in to school. And I would definitely be required to meet with a therapist. But none of that happened at the time. Instead, I was celebrated for the story, receiving a level of affirmation for it like almost nothing I had done before.

I'm sure it's one of the many reasons why I write today, I'm chasing that feeling over and over again.

I also still think about suicide, but not just because I want to make sense of why others see it as their only option. Apparently this was always the case though, I just didn't allow myself to realize it until now.

POWDER BLUE POLYESTER TUXEDO

There is quiet. Can you hear it? Just wait a moment. Pause. Take it in.

There is no screaming about toys, Animal Jam, showers, homework, dishes, screen time, or even screaming about why someone is screaming.

No one is complaining, crying, wheezing, moaning, grousing, grumbling, protesting, or bleating.

And no one is watching *Pokemon*, *Pretty Little Liars*, *Kicking It*, *H2O*, *The Fosters*, *America's Got Talent*, or *The X Factor*.

It is quiet, and it is like magic.

It is magic.

Noah, the little one, is lying on his back, brow furrowed, skin as buttery as ever, and he is reading *Miss Daisy is Crazy!*, one of the 20 million books in the *My Weird*

School series by my new best friend Dan Gutman. Other titles include *Mr. Klutz is Nuts!* and *Mrs. Roopy is Loopy!*, and on and on, ad infinitum.

Myles, the older one, is sprawled out on his stomach in our bed, his spiky, mushroom cap hair flying in 50 directions all at once, his long legs splayed everywhere, and he is re-reading, yes, you read that correctly, re-reading *Insurgent*, a book that couldn't be more in synch with what he loves—scrappy, underdog, outcast girl discovers she is special and then kicks all kinds of butt.

There was a time, what, last week maybe, when they considered reading to be a punishment, which maybe it was. We make them read every day, and at times we have made them do so when neither could find anything else to do, but fight with one another.

When I was their age I hung around the library, running my fingers along the spines of the books, lost in the covers, titles, and the endless possibilities lined-up neatly before me—*Dinkey Hocker Shoots Smack. I am the Baboon. Flowers in the Attic. The Chocolate War. The Outsiders. The Hobbit. The Martian Chronicles.*

I would check out four or five books at a time and I would consume them, the words like the candy I shoplifted back then, chewy, sweet, life affirming, and necessary.

One time when Myles was two years-old, we took him to

a party at a friend's house. The other children were doing what two year-olds do, dancing, jumping, running, crying, everything one can engage in while not exactly playing together. I watched Myles leave our side and weave his way through the masses before him. He avoided every kid in his path and made a bee-line for the bookshelf. Once there he proceeded to pull all of the children's books off of the shelf and then sat there in the middle of the pile, looking at each, one by one as the party went on around him.

This was amazing to watch, and something I felt proud of in its own weird anti-social way. But it didn't linger, this love of books was something brief, a blip, and maybe looking back, it wasn't about books anyway, but crowds, chaos and the anxieties that come with them.

I don't know, but I do know that I want him, and Noah to read, and to love reading, and while the feeling is desperate, and embarrassing, few things have meant more to me.

When I was their age, I read at the dinner table.

I read in museums my family visited, stretched out on the long black, leather couches.

I read on car trips, carrying a flashlight with me, so I wouldn't have to stop.

I read to fill time and space; to avoid my parent's never-ending dialogue about art and politics and everything in between; and to keep the voices in my head telling me I was loser with at bay.

I read to escape all of it, and everything, the confusion, the anger, the noise, and the desperate need to understand how things work, and don't, especially relationships, both my parents and mine; and to find some kind of peace, or at least some semblance of it.

And I still do.

"I only get to see my kid for like 30 minutes a day after work," the young guy behind the counter at the pizza place in our neighborhood says to me one day when I walk-in and the small talk has run its course, "his mom and I are not so cool right now."

"I'm sorry," I say.

"Yeah," he says, "thanks. Anyway, what should I do? What would you do, if you only had 30 minutes a day with your kid?"

"I would read to him," I say, "even 20 minutes of reading a day is great for brain development."

I might be bound to say something like this regardless of what may be the actual truth, but this is the truth, and there is science to back it up.

"Really?" he says incredulously.

"Really," I say, "it's like magic, but it isn't, its science, I promise."

"Okay," he says, and after he fills my order he gets on

his bike and rides away.

The first book I ever read cover to cover was a collection of Family Circus cartoons. You may know them. There is a mom and a dad, who doesn't seem to have any eyes. There are the kids, Billy, Dolly, Jeffy and PJ, the baby. There are also the "not me" ghosts, and a maybe not so subtle religious context that is more obvious to me now that I read *Family Circus* with the boys.

People tell me they hate Family Circus. It's too traditional, too retro and 1950's, with the stay at home mom and the dad shuffling to and from the office. And I get all of that, but back then, when I was kid, I didn't think about it.

What I knew then, was that I was just starting to read and it was the book I picked-up one morning instead of turning on the television as I lounged in our basement surrounded by the dark, barn wood walls my dad put in.

Soon page after page began to fly by, and I started to get scared.

It was like the time I road my bike up the street by my house and I decided it was finally time to go passed the speed limit sign at the top of the hill, an act that even then I knew was a kind of demarcation between childhood and something else—what comes next, knowledge, independence and facing what I feared.

—

On the other side of the sign, and down the steep hill that awaited me there, was a ravine. It was dark, and there was blind curve, but if you made it, a whole new world opened-up to you.

I had been scared to pass that sign, just as I was now scared to finish the book. What would happen when I did? It turns out that nothing happened, and everything.

There were no balloons or cheering fans when I reached that last page, just as there were no dragons or pots of gold awaiting me when I rode down the hill and by the ravine. But I also learned that doing these things were possible and real and that having tasted them, there was no turning back.

When I was little and I could not sleep unless my father read to me, book after book, *Ferdinand*, *Flat Stanley*, and so on. And when he ran out of books he went to the library and read about stories he could tell me, Czar Trojan and his goat's ears, and Ooka the Wise, the greatest judge in Old Japan. When he ran out of those, he made up stories about the ravens that cross over from the other side carrying messages from those we've lost.

Then I started to read myself, and I didn't need him anymore, but he had done his job.

I tried to do the same with the boys, reading them the endless books that flowed into the house, telling stories, and talking about books, always, and yet something didn't seem to be working, and I never understood why.

"He only wants to read comic books and graphic novels," we say to Myles teacher.

This is something that I could have never have predicted I would perceive as a problem before I became a parent, and I'm not even sure I think it is now as we ask the teacher about it. It's just that, he should at least read some books at least some of the time, right?

"But he's reading," she says.

She is kindly. She cares about him and teaching.

"He is," we say.

"Don't worry about it then," she says.

When I was twelve I was given a copy of *The Basketball Diaries* and it was so electric and full of pulsating energy, it nearly imploded in my hands. The characters were alive, they had dimension, and vibrancy; the action was real time, the rooftop masturbation, the basketball, and New York City this throbbing mass of concrete and thrills. And then there were the girls, the drugs, the sex, and sex abuse, and I don't know what I thought it meant to me then, but I know it meant that people must actually live like that, and that whether or not I was ever going to live like that myself, I wanted to at least somehow have the feeling again of what it felt like to read about it for the first time.

I still want that today, but now I want it for my children as well. How can't they want it too? And why isn't it automatic? I just don't get it. But that's the thing. So much of what we want to happen to our children when we are parents, crawling, walking, running, talking and on and on, is so confusing, and we never know how or when it will start, and when it does start, it seems like magic.

We don't know why it's happening. It just does when it does.

When I was a child there was a local children's entertainer named Todd the Magician. He played at children's parties, including mine. He wore a powder blue polyester tuxedo, a ruffled white shirt and an enormous black bow tie.

Todd didn't make the Statue of Liberty disappear, hang himself in a coffin from some tall building, or wrap himself in a straight jacket and allow people to throw him in the Susquehanna River so he could dramatically escape as his oxygen grew increasingly low and desperate.

But none of that mattered, because he performed magic, actual magic, all full of twisty balloons, endless scarves, shiny rings and sleight of hand.

There was nothing, and then there was something, or there was something, and then nothing, but regardless, something happened while Todd just stood there, smiling, magnificent, and God-like.

Or at least as God-like as one can be in a powder blue polyester tuxedo on a hot June day.

It helped of course to not try and figure out what he was doing, to just be in the moment, and that was fine with me. Unlike real life, I never cared how magic worked, just as I never really cared then, or now, how you can climb into a metal cylinder, sit there as it leaves the ground and then read a book as it takes you from one place to another. It was what it was, or it is what it is, unlike the relationships I could never quite understand, I accepted that if you suspended your doubts and fears about most everything else, believed in magic, and trusted that things would work out as they are supposed to, they would.

Not always mind you, but much of the time.

So, when you take-off from JFK, your plane stays in the air as the houses grow smaller, the earth begins to look like a series of interlocking grids, and the lakes give away to mountains. And then you are suddenly landing at LAX, where the sky is always blue and the chance for magic happening feels palpable and endless.

Like any relationship, parenting doesn't always feel like that though, not in the moment anyway, and not until it does, but it will, eventually, and much of the time anyway.

And so, on this day there is quiet.

Can you hear it?

Just wait a moment.

Pause.

Take it in.

It is like magic. It is magic.

The boys are reading and not because we made them do so, or because it is so important to me. It is because developmentally they have caught up with my needs and impatience, and my inability to accept that unlike actual magic, when it comes to parenting, things happen as they are supposed to if you remain diligent and trust in their inevitability.

As important as all of that, there is also the fact that the boys have found things they like, and that speak to them. They have their *Family Circus* and *The Basketball Diaries*.

A switch has flipped, and some bizzarro sleight of hand has occurred right in front of me. There was nothing, but now there is something.

There is reading.

And so maybe it isn't actually magic, but it sure feels like it.

ACKNOWLEDGMENTS

There is no book without the Dane Bahr and Dock Street Press and I want to thank the whole team for making it real. I also want to thank Sarah Lippmann and Robert James Russell, because they lit the path that I joyfully stumbled down.

I need to thank so many wonderful journals and sites for running so many of these pieces in one form or another—*The Rumpus, Nailed, TNBBC, Thought Catalog, decomP,* The *Weeklings, Manifest-Station, Collected Poop Stories* (for real), *Midnight Mind, RAGAD, Entropy, Revolution John, CCLaP* and *Rated Rookie,* as well as the kick-ass editors who were so encouraging along the way—Gina Frangello, Sean Beaudoin, Nick Ostdick, Brett Van Emst, Joshua M. Bernstein, Zoe Zolbrod, Greg Olear, Jen Pastiloff, Matty Byloos,

Shay DeGrandis, Sheldon Lee Compton, John Wentworth Chapin, Jason Pettus and Lori Hettler.

I also want to thank my wife Debbie, the boys Myles and Noah, my mom Judy and brother Adam, great supporters all, and attractive and funny too, which is nice.

Not to mention Adam Lawrence and Eric Boime who go way back to the beginning of time and have their finger-prints and DNA all over much of the memories and milestones contained herein.

And most finally, all the quite fine essayists and memoirists who I love, though none more than Megan Stielstra and Wendy C. Ortiz.

Ben Tanzer is the author of the books *Orphans*, which won the 24th Annual Midwest Book Award in Fantasy/SciFi/Horror/Paranormal and a· Bronze medal in the Science Fiction category at the 2015 IPPY Awards, *Lost in Space*, which received the 2015 Devil's Kitchen Reading Award in Prose Nonfiction, *The New York Stories* and *SEX AND DEATH*. He has also contributed to *Punk Planet*, *Clamor*, and *Men's Health*, serves as Senior Director, Acquisitions for Curbside Splendor, frequently speaks on the topics of messaging, framing, social media, blogging, fiction, essay writing and independent publishing and can be found online at tanzerben.com the center of his vast lifestyle empire.